© Copyright 2021 Raymond Cook - All Rights Reserved.

In no way is it legal to reproduce, duplicate, or transmit any part of thi means or in printed format. Recording of this publication is strictly pr......, ... storage of this material is not allowed unless with written permission from the publisher. All rights reserved.

The information provided herein is stated to be truthful and consistent, in that any liability, regarding inattention or otherwise, by any usage or abuse of any policies, processes, or directions contained within is the solitary and complete responsibility of the recipient reader. Under no circumstances will any legal liability or blame be held against the publisher for any reparation, damages, or monetary loss due to the information herein, either directly or indirectly.

Respective authors own all copyrights not held by the publisher.

Legal Notice:
This book is copyright protected. This is only for personal use. You cannot amend, distribute, sell, use, quote or paraphrase any part of the content within this book without the consent of the author or copyright owner. Legal action will be pursued if this is breached.

Disclaimer Notice:
Please note the information contained within this document is for educational and entertainment purposes only. Every attempt has been made to provide accurate, up-to-date and reliable, complete information. No warranties of any kind are expressed or implied. Readers acknowledge that the author is not engaging in the rendering of legal, financial, medical or professional advice.

By reading this document, the reader agrees that under no circumstances are we responsible for any losses, direct or indirect, which are incurred as a result of the use of information contained within this document, including, but not limited to, errors, omissions, or inaccuracies.

CONTENTS

DIABETES DIET, EATING, & PHYSICAL ACTIVITY 6

What foods can I eat if I have diabetes? 6

What foods and drinks should I limit if I have diabetes? 7

When should I eat if I have diabetes? 8

Will supplements and vitamins help my diabetes? 8

Why should I be physically active if I have diabetes? 8

How can I be physically active safely if I have diabetes? 9

What physical activities should I do if I have diabetes? 10

14-Day Meal Plan 12

HEALTHY BREAKFAST RECIPES 13

Eggs And Tomato 13

Beef With Dried Apricots 14

Amaranth Porridge 15

Spanish Eggs 16

Coconut Cabbage Mix 17

Oats & Millet Porridge 18

Eggs And Mushroom 19

Banana Pancakes 20

Tomato Basil Frittata 21

LOW CARB LUNCH & DINNER RECIPES 22

Vegetables In Half And Half 22

Roast Vegetable And Bean Stew 23

Instant Pot Cinnamon Apricot And Pears 24

Beansprout Soup 25

Kale Sausage Stew 26

Glazed Carrots And Cauliflower 27

Creamy Broccoli And Ham 28

Chick Pea Curry 29

Italian Beef Roast 30

POULTRY RECIPES **31**

Lemon Cilantro Chicken 31

Chicken Tacos 32

Chicken & Beans Chili 34

Sausage And Cauliflower "grits" 35

Instant Pot Chicken Breast 36

Moroccan Chicken Bowls 37

Thai Green Turkey Curry 39

Chicken Coconut Curry 40

Chicken Stuffed Potatoes 41

BEEF PORK & LAMB RECIPES **42**

Lamb Chops With Beans & Spinach 42

Fabada 43

Veal In Milk 44

Oxtail Soup 45

Beef Goulash 46

Fruity Pork Loin 47

5-ingredient Mexican Lasagna 48

FISH AND SEAFOOD RECIPES **49**

Rosemary Salmon 49

Swordfish Steak 50

Shrimp With Tomatoes And Feta 51

Sardine Curry 52

Shrimp Coconut Curry 53

Sweet & Sour Tuna 54

Coconut Shrimp Curry 55

Salmon In Green Sauce 56

VEGAN AND VEGETABLE RECIPES 57

Squash Medley 57

Split Pea Stew 58

Eggplant Curry 59

Seitan Roast 60

Chili Sin Carne 61

Lentil And Eggplant Stew 62

Seitan Curry 63

Mango Tofu Curry 64

SOUPS & STEWS RECIPES 65

Kidney Bean Stew 65

Sweet And Sour Soup 66

Egg Salad 67

Chili Con Carne 68

Zucchini Soup 69

Irish Beef Stew 70

Spicy Pepper Soup 71

Broccoli Stilton Soup 72

DESSERTS RECIPES 73

Spiced Pear Applesauce 73

Crustless Key Lime Cheesecake 74

Brownies 76

Egg Custard 77

Chia Pudding With Mango 78

Vanilla Mug Cake 79

Oatmeal Bites 80

Apple And Cinnamon Cake 81

APPETIZERS AND SNACKS 82

Candied Walnuts 82

Mushroom Tofu Scramble 83

Mushroom And Eggs 84

Sweet Potato Fries 85

Cilantro Lime Drumsticks 86

Eggplant Tofu Scramble 87

Spinach Dip 88

Mushroom Tofu Scramble 89

SIDE DISHES RECIPES 90

Rosemary Potatoes 90

Lemon Hummus 91

Chili Lime Salmon 92

Chili Greens 93

Lemony Brussels Sprouts With Poppy Seeds 94

Tuna Melt 95

Quinoa Tabbouleh 96

Low Fat Roasties 97

OTHER TYPE 2 DIABETES RECIPES 98

Poached Peaches 98

Vanilla And Pumpkin Pudding 99

Instant Pot Salmon With Jalapeno 100

Roasted Tomatillo Salsa 101

Herbed Turkey Breast With Butter Gravy 102

Keto Instant Pot Chunky Chili 103

Chicken Bone Broth 104

Blue Cheese And Pear Melts 105

RECIPES INDEX 106

DIABETES DIET, EATING, & PHYSICAL ACTIVITY

Nutrition and physical activity are important parts of a healthy lifestyle when you have diabetes. Along with other benefits, following a healthy meal plan and being active can help you keep your blood glucose level, also called blood sugar, in your target range. To manage your blood glucose, you need to balance what you eat and drink with physical activity and diabetes medicine, if you take any. What you choose to eat, how much you eat, and when you eat are all important in keeping your blood glucose level in the range that your health care team recommends.

Becoming more active and making changes in what you eat and drink can seem challenging at first. You may find it easier to start with small changes and get help from your family, friends, and health care team.

Eating well and being physically active most days of the week can help you
keep your blood glucose level, blood pressure, and cholesterol in your target ranges
lose weight or stay at a healthy weight
prevent or delay diabetes problems
feel good and have more energy

What foods can I eat if I have diabetes?

You may worry that having diabetes means going without foods you enjoy. The good news is that you can still eat your favorite foods, but you might need to eat smaller portions or enjoy them less often. Your health care team will help create a diabetes meal plan for you that meets your needs and likes.

The key to eating with diabetes is to eat a variety of healthy foods from all food groups, in the amounts your meal plan outlines.
The food groups are

vegetables
- nonstarchy: includes broccoli, carrots, greens, peppers, and tomatoes
- starchy: includes potatoes, corn, and green peas

fruits—includes oranges, melon, berries, apples, bananas, and grapes

grains—at least half of your grains for the day should be whole grains
- includes wheat, rice, oats, cornmeal, barley, and quinoa

- examples: bread, pasta, cereal, and tortillas

protein
- lean meat
- chicken or turkey without the skin
- fish
- eggs
- nuts and peanuts
- dried beans and certain peas, such as chickpeas and split peas
- meat substitutes, such as tofu

dairy—nonfat or low fat
- milk or lactose-free milk if you have lactose intolerance
- yogurt
- cheese

<u>Eat foods with heart-healthy fats, which mainly come from these foods:</u>
- oils that are liquid at room temperature, such as canola and olive oil
- nuts and seeds
- heart-healthy fish such as salmon, tuna, and mackerel
- avocado

Use oils when cooking food instead of butter, cream, shortening, lard, or stick margarine.

What foods and drinks should I limit if I have diabetes?

<u>Foods and drinks to limit include</u>
- fried foods and other foods high in saturated fat and trans fat
- foods high in salt, also called sodium
- sweets, such as baked goods, candy, and ice cream
- beverages with added sugars, such as juice, regular soda, and regular sports or energy drinks

Drink water instead of sweetened beverages. Consider using a sugar substitute in your coffee or tea.

If you drink alcohol, drink moderately—no more than one drink a day if you're a woman or two drinks a day if you're a man. If you use insulin or diabetes medicines that increase the amount of insulin your body makes, alcohol can make your blood glucose level drop too low. This is especially true if you haven't eaten in a while. It's best to eat some food when you drink alcohol.

When should I eat if I have diabetes?

Some people with diabetes need to eat at about the same time each day. Others can be more flexible with the timing of their meals. Depending on your diabetes medicines or type of insulin, you may need to eat the same amount of carbohydrates at the same time each day. If you take "mealtime" insulin, your eating schedule can be more flexible.

If you use certain diabetes medicines or insulin and you skip or delay a meal, your blood glucose level can drop too low. Ask your health care team when you should eat and whether you should eat before and after physical activity.

Will supplements and vitamins help my diabetes?

No clear proof exists that taking dietary supplements such as vitamins, minerals, herbs, or spices can help manage diabetes. You may need supplements if you cannot get enough vitamins and minerals from foods. Talk with your health care provider before you take any dietary supplement since some can cause side effects or affect how your medicines work.

Why should I be physically active if I have diabetes?

Physical activity is an important part of managing your blood glucose level and staying healthy. Being active has many health benefits.

<u>Physical activity</u>

- lowers blood glucose levels
- lowers blood pressure
- improves blood flow
- burns extra calories so you can keep your weight down if needed
- improves your mood
- can prevent falls and improve memory in older adults
- may help you sleep better

If you are overweight, combining physical activity with a reduced-calorie eating plan can lead to even more benefits. In the Look AHEAD: Action for Health in Diabetes study,1 overweight adults with type 2 diabetes who ate less and moved more had greater long-term health benefits compared to those who didn't make these changes. These benefits included improved cholesterol levels, less sleep apnea, and being able to move around more easily.

Even small amounts of physical activity can help. Experts suggest that you aim for at least 30 minutes of moderate or vigorous physical activity 5 days of the week. Moderate activity feels somewhat hard, and vigorous activity is intense and feels hard. If you want to lose weight or maintain weight loss, you may need to do 60 minutes or more of physical activity 5 days of the week.

Be patient. It may take a few weeks of physical activity before you see changes in your health.

How can I be physically active safely if I have diabetes?

Be sure to drink water before, during, and after exercise to stay well hydrated. The following are some other tips for safe physical activity when you have diabetes.

1. Plan ahead

Talk with your health care team before you start a new physical activity routine, especially if you have other health problems. Your health care team will tell you a target range for your blood glucose level and suggest how you can be active safely.

Your health care team also can help you decide the best time of day for you to do physical activity based on your daily schedule, meal plan, and diabetes medicines. If you take insulin, you need to balance the activity that you do with your insulin doses and meals so you don't get low blood glucose.

2. Prevent low blood glucose

Because physical activity lowers your blood glucose, you should protect yourself against low blood glucose levels, also called hypoglycemia. You are most likely to have hypoglycemia if you take insulin or certain other diabetes medicines, such as a sulfonylurea. Hypoglycemia also can occur after a long intense workout or if you have skipped a meal before being active. Hypoglycemia can happen during or up to 24 hours after physical activity.

Planning is key to preventing hypoglycemia. For instance, if you take insulin, your health care provider might suggest you take less insulin or eat a small snack with carbohydrates before, during, or after physical activity, especially intense activity.4

You may need to check your blood glucose level before, during, and right after you are physically active.

3. Stay safe when blood glucose is high

If you have type 1 diabetes, avoid vigorous physical activity when you have ketones in your blood or urine. Ketones are chemicals your body might make when your blood glucose level is too high, a condition called hyperglycemia, and your insulin level is too low. If you are physically active when you have ketones in your blood or urine, your blood glucose level may go even higher. Ask your health care team what level of ketones are dangerous for you and how to test for them. Ketones are uncommon in people with type 2 diabetes.

4. Take care of your feet

People with diabetes may have problems with their feet because of poor blood flow and nerve damage that can result from high blood glucose levels. To help prevent foot problems, you should wear comfortable, supportive shoes and take care of your feet before, during, and after physical activity.

What physical activities should I do if I have diabetes?

Most kinds of physical activity can help you take care of your diabetes. Certain activities may be unsafe for some people, such as those with low vision or nerve damage to their feet. Ask your health care team what physical activities are safe for you. Many people choose walking with friends or family members for their activity.

Doing different types of physical activity each week will give you the most health benefits. Mixing it up also helps reduce boredom and lower your chance of getting hurt. Try these options for physical activity.

Add extra activity to your daily routine

If you have been inactive or you are trying a new activity, start slowly, with 5 to 10 minutes a day. Then add a little more time each week. Increase daily activity by spending less time in front of a TV or other screen. Try these simple ways to add physical activities in your life each day:

- Walk around while you talk on the phone or during TV commercials.
- Do chores, such as work in the garden, rake leaves, clean the house, or wash the car.
- Park at the far end of the shopping center parking lot and walk to the store.
- Take the stairs instead of the elevator.
- Make your family outings active, such as a family bike ride or a walk in a park.

If you are sitting for a long time, such as working at a desk or watching TV, do some light activity for 3 minutes or more every half hour.5 Light activities include
- leg lifts or extensions
- overhead arm stretches
- desk chair swivels
- torso twists

- side lunges
- walking in place

Do aerobic exercise

Aerobic exercise is activity that makes your heart beat faster and makes you breathe harder. You should aim for doing aerobic exercise for 30 minutes a day most days of the week. You do not have to do all the activity at one time. You can split up these minutes into a few times throughout the day.

To get the most out of your activity, exercise at a moderate to vigorous level. Try

- walking briskly or hiking
- climbing stairs
- swimming or a water-aerobics class
- dancing
- riding a bicycle or a stationary bicycle
- taking an exercise class
- playing basketball, tennis, or other sports

Talk with your health care team about how to warm up and cool down before and after you exercise.

Do strength training to build muscle

Strength training is a light or moderate physical activity that builds muscle and helps keep your bones healthy. Strength training is important for both men and women. When you have more muscle and less body fat, you'll burn more calories. Burning more calories can help you lose and keep off extra weight.

You can do strength training with hand weights, elastic bands, or weight machines. Try to do strength training two to three times a week. Start with a light weight. Slowly increase the size of your weights as your muscles become stronger.

Do stretching exercises

Stretching exercises are light or moderate physical activity. When you stretch, you increase your flexibility, lower your stress, and help prevent sore muscles.

You can choose from many types of stretching exercises. Yoga is a type of stretching that focuses on your breathing and helps you relax. Even if you have problems moving or balancing, certain types of yoga can help. For instance, chair yoga has stretches you can do when sitting in a chair or holding onto a chair while standing. Your health care team can suggest whether yoga is right for you.

14-Day Meal Plan

Meal Plan	Breakfast	Lunch	Dinner
Day-1	Eggs And Tomato	Vegetables In Half And Half	Kidney Bean Stew
Day-2	Beef With Dried Apricots	Roast Vegetable And Bean Stew	Lamb Chops With Beans & Spinach
Day-3	Amaranth Porridge	Italian Beef Roast	Lemon Cilantro Chicken
Day-4	Spanish Eggs	Glazed Carrots And Cauliflower	Shrimp Coconut Curry
Day-5	Coconut Cabbage Mix	Sausage And Cauliflower "grits"	Beansprout Soup
Day-6	Oats & Millet Porridge	Chili Lime Salmon	Chicken & Beans Chili
Day-7	Eggs And Mushroom	Kale Sausage Stew	Salmon In Green Sauce
Day-8	Banana Pancakes	Chili Con Carne	Creamy Broccoli And Ham
Day-9	Tomato Basil Frittata	Eggplant Tofu Scramble	Mushroom Tofu Scramble
Day-10	Chicken Tacos	Instant Pot Chicken Breast	Chicken Bone Broth
Day-11	Apple And Cinnamon Cake	Instant Pot Salmon With Jalapeno	Beef Goulash
Day-12	Oatmeal Bites	Thai Green Turkey Curry	Tuna Melt
Day-13	Crustless Key Lime Cheesecake	Split Pea Stew	Moroccan Chicken Bowls
Day-14	Egg Custard	Rosemary Salmon	Blue Cheese And Pear Melts

HEALTHY BREAKFAST RECIPES

Eggs And Tomato

Servings: 2
Cooking Time: 7 Minutes

Ingredients:

- 3 eggs
- ¼ cup milk
- 1 cup chopped cherry tomatoes
- 1 tsp. mixed herbs
- 1/2 tsp. Salt

Directions:

1. Spray a heat-proof bowl that fits in your Instant Pot with nonstick spray.
2. Whisk together the eggs, milk, salt, and herbs.
3. Pour into the bowl. Add the tomatoes. Place the bowl in your steamer basket.
4. Pour 1 cup of water into your Instant Pot. Lower the basket into your Instant Pot.
5. Seal and cook on low pressure for 7 minutes. Depressurize quickly.
6. Stir well and allow to rest, it will finish cooking in its own heat.

Nutrition:

- InfoCalories 110, Carbs 5g, Fat 8g, Protein 16g, Potassium (K)379 mg, Sodium (Na) 513 mg

Beef With Dried Apricots

Servings: 4
Cooking Time: 60 Minutes

Ingredients:
- 2 cups dried apricots
- 2 teaspoons garlic powder
- Salt and black pepper, to taste
- 1 teaspoon coriander, ground
- 3 cups beef stock
- 2.5 pounds beef brisket, boneless

Directions:
1. Dump the listed ingredients in the instant pot.
2. Press meat stew button and cook on high for 60 minutes. Once timer beeps, release steam naturally for 15 minutes. Open the pot and stir. Serve.

Amaranth Porridge

Servings: 4
Cooking Time: 6 Minutes

Ingredients:
- 1 cup amaranth
- 2 cups water
- ¼ cup fresh raspberries
- 3-4 drops liquid stevia
- Pinch of salt

Directions:
1. In the pot of Instant Pot, place the water, amaranth and salt and mix well.
2. Close the lid and place the pressure valve to "Seal" position.
3. Press "Manual" and cook under "High Pressure" for about 6 minutes.
4. Press "Cancel" and carefully allow a "Quick" release.
5. Open the lid and stir in stevia.
6. Serve warm with the topping of raspberries.

Nutrition:
- Info Per serving:Calories: 186, Fats: 3.2g, Carbs: 33.1g, Sugar: 1.2g, Proteins: 7.1g, Sodium: 53mg

Spanish Eggs

Servings: 2
Cooking Time: 7 Minutes

Ingredients:

- 3 eggs
- ¼ cup milk
- 1 cup shredded, fried onion
- 1 tsp. smoked paprika
- 1/2 tsp. Salt

Directions:

1. Spray a heat-proof bowl that fits in your Instant Pot with nonstick spray.
2. Whisk together the eggs, milk, salt, and paprika.
3. Pour into the bowl. Add the onion. Place the bowl in your steamer basket.
4. Pour 1 cup of water into your Instant Pot. Lower the basket into your Instant Pot.
5. Seal and cook on low pressure for 7 minutes. Depressurize quickly.
6. Stir well and allow to rest, it will finish cooking in its own heat.

Nutrition:

- InfoCalories 125, Carbs 5g, Fat 8g, Protein 16g, Potassium (K) 1001 mg, Sodium (Na) 467.1 mg

Coconut Cabbage Mix

Servings: 1
Cooking Time: 5 Minutes

Ingredients:

- 4 tablespoons of coconut oil
- 1 small onion, sliced
- Salt and black pepper, to taste
- ½ teaspoon of garlic, minced
- 1 -1/2 cups cabbage, sliced
- 1/3 cup coconut milk, unsweetened

Directions:

1. Turn on the sauté mode. Add coconut oil to the instant pot and let it get hot.
2. Add onions and cook until translucent. Next, add salt, black pepper, garlic, and cook.
3. Then add cabbage and ¼ amount of coconut milk, and cook for 1 minute.
4. Lock the lid and set the timer to 2 minutes at low pressure.
5. After 2 minutes quick release the steam.
6. Then press the keep warm button and pour the remaining coconut milk.
7. Stir for 4 minutes. Serve hot and enjoy.

Oats & Millet Porridge

Servings: 5
Cooking Time: 12 Minutes

Ingredients:
- ¾ cup dry millet
- ½ cup rolled oats
- 2 apples, cored and chopped
- 3 cups water
- 1 teaspoon olive oil
- 1 teaspoon ground cinnamon
- ½ teaspoon ground ginger

Directions:
1. In the Instant Pot, place oil and press "Sauté". Then add millet and cook for about 1-2 minutes or until fragrant, stirring continuously.
2. Press "Cancel" and stir in the remaining ingredients.
3. Close the lid and place the pressure valve to "Seal" position.
4. Press "Manual" and cook under "High Pressure" for about 10 minutes.
5. Press "Cancel" and allow a "Natural" release for about 15 minutes. Then allow a "Quick" release.
6. Open the lid and with a spoon, stir the mixture well.
7. Serve warm.

Nutrition:
- Info Per serving:Calories: 201, Fats: 2.9g, Carbs: 40.1g, Sugar: 9g, Proteins: 4.7g, Sodium: 7mg

Eggs And Mushroom

Servings: 2
Cooking Time: 7 Minutes

Ingredients:
- 3 eggs
- ¼ cup mushroom soup
- 1 cup chopped mushrooms
- 1 tsp. mixed herbs
- 1/2 tsp. Salt

Directions:
1. Spray a heat-proof bowl that fits in your Instant Pot with nonstick spray.
2. Whisk together the eggs, soup, salt, and herbs.
3. Pour into the bowl. Add the mushrooms. Place the bowl in your steamer basket.
4. Pour 1 cup of water into your Instant Pot. Lower the basket into your Instant Pot.
5. Seal and cook on low pressure for 7 minutes. Depressurize quickly.
6. Stir well and allow to rest, it will finish cooking in its own heat.

Nutrition:
- InfoCalories 100, Carbs 4g, Fat 8g, Protein 16g, Potassium (K)336 mg, Sodium (Na) 616 mg

Banana Pancakes

Servings: 2
Cooking Time: 15 Minutes

Ingredients:
- 1 medium banana, peeled
- 2 eggs

Directions:
1. Place banana in a food processor, add eggs and pulse for 1 minute or until smooth batter comes together.
2. Plugin instant pot, insert the inner pot, press sauté/simmer button, add oil and when hot, add 2 tablespoons of prepared batter for each pancake.
3. Cook pancakes for 2 minutes per side or until nicely golden brown and cooked through and when done, transfer pancakes to a plate.
4. Use remaining batter for cooking more pancakes and serve straightaway.

Nutrition:
- InfoCalories: 124 Cal, Carbs: 14 g, Fat: 5 g, Protein: 7 g, Fiber: 2 g.

Tomato Basil Frittata

Servings: 8

Cooking Time: 25 Minutes

Ingredients:

- 1 cup frozen spinach, thawed
- 1 sliced tomato
- 1 diced tomato
- 2 cups thawed hash browns
- ¼ teaspoon ground black pepper
- 2 teaspoons dried basil
- 6 eggs
- ¼ cup milk, non-fat
- ½ cup cheddar cheese, low-fat
- 1 ½ cups water

Directions:

1. Crack eggs in a bowl, add all the ingredients except for slice tomato and water and stir until combined.
2. Take a heatproof dish that fits into the instant pot, grease it with oil, then pour in the prepared batter and scatter sliced tomato on top.
3. Plugin instant pot, insert the inner pot, pour in water, then insert trivet stand and place dish on it.
4. Shut the instant pot with its lid and turn the pressure knob to seal the pot.
5. Press the 'manual' button, then press the 'timer' to set the cooking time to 20 minutes and cook at high pressure, instant pot will take 5 minutes or more for building its inner pressure.
6. When the timer beeps, press 'cancel' button and do quick pressure release until pressure nob drops down.
7. Open the instant pot, remove the dish from the instant pot, wipe any moisture from the top of frittata using paper towels, and serve.

Nutrition:

- InfoCalories: 129 Cal, Carbs: 2 g, Fat: 8 g, Protein: 11 g, Fiber: 1.4 g.

LOW CARB LUNCH & DINNER RECIPES

Vegetables In Half And Half

Servings: 2
Cooking Time: 8 Minutes

Ingredients:
- 2 medium parsnips, peeled and cubed
- 1 fennel bulb, sliced
- 3 cloves garlic, minced
- 1 cup chicken broth
- 1 cup half-and-half
- Salt and pepper, to taste

Directions:
1. Add fennel bulbs, parsnip, chicken broth, garlic, salt, and pepper into the instant pot.
2. Lock the lid of the pot. Set timer for 5 minutes at high pressure.
3. Once time beeps, quick release the steam. Turn on the sauté mode and reduce the liquid.
4. Stir occasionally. Next, add half and half and mix well.
5. Stir for 2 more minutes and then serve the dish hot. Enjoy.

Roast Vegetable And Bean Stew

Servings: 6
Cooking Time: 10 Minutes

Ingredients:
- 19-ounce cooked pinto beans
- 1 small butternut squash
- 1-pound potatoes
- 2 large zucchinis
- 2 medium carrots
- 2 medium parsnips
- 1 teaspoon minced garlic
- 1 ½ teaspoon salt
- ¾ teaspoon ground black pepper
- 4 large sprigs of rosemary
- 1 cup apple cider
- 2 teaspoons olive oil
- 1 cup vegetable broth

Directions:
1. Peel squash, potatoes, zucchini, carrot, and parsnips, then cut into 1 ½ inch pieces and place into the inner pot of instant pot.
2. Plugin instant pot, add remaining ingredients except for beans and stir until mixed, then shut the instant pot with its lid and turn the pressure knob to seal the pot.
3. Press the 'manual' button, then press the 'timer' to set the cooking time to 3 minutes and cook at high pressure, instant pot will take 5 minutes or more for building its inner pressure.
4. When the timer beeps, press 'cancel' button and do quick pressure release until pressure nob drops down.
5. Open the instant pot, add kidney beans, stir until well mixed, then shut instant pot with a lid and let rest for 10 minutes.
6. Serve straight away.

Nutrition:
- InfoCalories: 278 Cal, Carbs: 58 g, Fat: 3 g, Protein: 8 g, Fiber: 11 g.

Instant Pot Cinnamon Apricot And Pears

Servings: 3
Cooking Time: 5 Minutes

Ingredients:

- ¼ cup of lime juice
- 2 apricot peeled
- 1 teaspoon of cinnamon
- 2 pears, peeled
- Salt, pinch
- 2 scoops of stevia powder

Directions:

1. Peel, core, and slice the fruits. Transfer the apricot, cinnamon, pears, salt, and stevia in the instant pot. Pour the lime juice in the instant pot.
2. Lock the lid of the instant pot, and set the timer to 2 minutes at high pressure.
3. Once timer beeps, release the steam quickly. Turn on the sauté mode and reduce the liquid.
4. Serve immediately and enjoy.

Beansprout Soup

Servings: 2
Cooking Time: 10 Minutes

Ingredients:
- 1lb beansprouts
- 1lb chopped vegetables
- 1 cup low sodium broth
- 1tbsp mixed herbs
- 1 minced onion

Directions:
1. Mix all the ingredients in your Instant Pot.
2. Cook on Stew for 10 minutes.
3. Release the pressure naturally.

Nutrition:
- Info Per serving:Calories: 100;Carbs: 4 ;Sugar: 1 ;Fat: 10 ;Protein: 4 ;GL: 2

Kale Sausage Stew

Servings: 2
Cooking Time: 10 Minutes

Ingredients:
- 1lb cooked chopped sausage
- 1lb shredded kale
- 1 cup vegetable broth
- 1tbsp mixed herbs
- 1tbsp gravy

Directions:
1. Mix all the ingredients in your Instant Pot.
2. Cook on Stew for 10 minutes.
3. Release the pressure naturally.

Nutrition:
- Info Per serving:Calories: 300;Carbs: 9 ;Sugar: 1 ;Fat: 20 ;Protein: 30 ;GL: 3

Glazed Carrots And Cauliflower

Servings: 2
Cooking Time: 5 Minutes

Ingredients:
- 1/3 pound of baby carrot
- 1 cauliflower head, small and chopped
- 3⁄4 cup lime juice
- 3 tablespoons butter/olive oil
- 1/3 cup stevia
- 1⁄4 teaspoon ground cinnamon
- Salt and black pepper, to taste

Directions:
1. Combine all the ingredients in the instant pot. Lock the lid and set the timer to 5 minutes.
2. Open timer beeps, release the steam quickly. Open the instant pot lid. Stir and serve.

Creamy Broccoli And Ham

Servings: 4

Cooking Time: 10 Minutes

Ingredients:

- 20 ounces of broccoli
- 12 ounces of ham, smoked and chopped
- 8 ounces of fat-free cream of mushroom soup
- 1 cup almond milk
- 2 cups of Cheddar cheese, shredded
- Salt and black pepper
- 2 teaspoons of olive oil

Directions:

1. Turn on the sauté mode of the instant pot. Add oil and heat it.
2. Then add broccoli and cook for one minute. Next, add ham and season it with salt and pepper. Pour in the cream of mushroom soup and almond milk and lock the lid.
3. Set timer for 4 minutes at high pressure. Once timer beeps, quick release the steam.
4. Reduce the liquid by turning on the sauté mode. Keep stirring.
5. After a few mins, add cheese and cook for 2 minutes at sauté mode. Once it's done serve.

Chick Pea Curry

Servings: 2
Cooking Time: 27 Minutes

Ingredients:

- 1 cup chickpeas, uncooked
- 1 chopped white onion
- 2 chopped green chilies
- 1 chopped tomato
- 2 tsps. minced garlic
- 1 tsp. grated ginger
- 1 tsp. salt
- 1 tsp. red chili powder
- 1 tsp. coriander powder
- 1 tsp. garam masala
- 1 tsp. turmeric powder
- 3 bay leaves
- 3 tbsps. olive oil
- 1 tbsp. chopped parsley
- 2 cups water

Directions:

1. Plugin instant pot, insert the inner pot, and add chickpeas and 1 ¼ cup water.
2. Shut the instant pot with its lid and turn the pressure knob to seal the pot.
3. Press the 'manual' button, then press the 'timer' to set the cooking time to 12 minutes and cook at high pressure, instant pot will take 5 minutes or more for building its inner pressure.
4. When the timer beeps, press 'cancel' button and do natural pressure release for 5 minutes and then do quick pressure release until pressure nob drops down.
5. Then open the instant pot, drain chickpeas, and set aside.
6. Place a skillet pan over medium heat, add oil and bay leaves and fry for 30 seconds.
7. Stir in ginger and garlic paste and cook for 1 minute or until nicely golden brown and fragrant.
8. Season with salt, chili powder, coriander, garam masala, and turmeric, continue cooking for 3 minutes, then pour in remaining water and bring the gravy to boil.
9. Then add cooked chickpeas, stir well, and cook for 5 minutes, covering the pan.
10. Serve straight away.

Nutrition:

- InfoCalories 212, Carbs 39g, Fat 3.6g, Protein 9.8g, Potassium (K) 387 mg, Sodium (Na) 836 mg

Italian Beef Roast

Servings: 5
Cooking Time: 70 Minutes

Ingredients:
- 4 pounds of beef roast
- 2 tablespoons of red pepper
- 4 tablespoons of garlic infused olive oil
- Salt and black pepper, to taste
- 20 ounces of Peperoncini
- 1 cup beef broth

Directions:
1. Take a plastic bag and place beef roast, red pepper, garlic infused oil, salt, and black pepper in it. Let it marinate for 30 minutes.
2. After marinating, add beef, a jar of the peperoncini and broth into the instant pot.
3. Set timer for 70 minutes at high pressure.
4. After 70 minutes, naturally, release the steam for 20 minutes.
5. Serve Beef in bowls and enjoy.

POULTRY RECIPES

Lemon Cilantro Chicken

Servings: 2
Cooking Time: 35 Minutes

Ingredients:

- 1lb diced chicken breast
- 1lb chopped vegetables
- 1 cup chicken broth
- juice of half a lemon
- 2tbsp dry cilantro

Directions:

1. Mix all the ingredients in your Instant Pot.
2. Cook on Stew for 35 minutes.
3. Release the pressure naturally.

Nutrition:

- Info Per serving:Calories: 280;Carbs: 4 ;Sugar: 0 ;Fat: 12 ;Protein: 45 ;GL: 1

Chicken Tacos

Servings: 10
Cooking Time: 25 Minutes

Ingredients:
- 4 pounds chicken breast
- 1/2 of a medium head of lettuce, shredded
- 3 medium avocados, pitted and flesh chopped
- 1 medium white onion, peeled and chopped
- 3 limes, juiced
- 2 jalapeno peppers, deseeded and diced
- 1 teaspoon onion powder
- 1 teaspoon garlic powder
- 1 ¾ teaspoon salt
- 1 teaspoon ground black pepper
- 1 ½ teaspoon red chili powder
- 1 ½ teaspoon ground cumin
- 2 tablespoons olive oil

Directions:

1. Place lettuce, avocado, onion, and pepper in a large bowl, drizzle with lime juice and toss until coated, chill vegetables in the refrigerator for 30 minutes.
2. Meanwhile, plug-in instant pot, insert the inner pot, pour in water, then insert trivet stand and place chicken on it.
3. Shut the instant pot with its lid, turn the pressure knob to seal the pot, press the 'manual' button, then press the 'timer' to set the cooking time to 10 minutes and cook at high pressure, instant pot will take 5 minutes or more for building its inner pressure.
4. When the timer beeps, press 'cancel' button and do quick pressure release until pressure nob drops down.
5. Open the instant pot, transfer chicken breasts to a cutting board, cool for 5 minutes, then shred with two forks.
6. Place shredded chicken in a bowl and season with salt, black pepper, red chili, and cumin until evenly coated.
7. Drain the instant pot, wipe clean the inner pot, then press the 'sauté/simmer' button, grease with oil and when hot, add seasoned chicken in a single layer and cook for 3 to 5 minutes or until chicken is nicely golden brown and slightly crispy.
8. Serve chicken in tortillas, topped with prepared vegetables.

Nutrition:

- InfoCalories: 164.4 Cal, Carbs: 8.3 g, Fat: 11.1 g, Protein: 10.1 g, Fiber: 4.8 g.

Chicken & Beans Chili

Servings: 4
Cooking Time: 13 Minutes

Ingredients:

- 1 pound boneless, skinless chicken breasts
- 30 ounces boiled white northern beans
- 2 jalapeño peppers, hopped
- 1 medium onion, chopped
- 3 cups low-sodium chicken broth
- 2 garlic cloves, minced
- 1 teaspoon dried oregano
- 1 teaspoon ground cumin
- ½ teaspoon red chili powder
- Ground black pepper, as required

Directions:

1. In the pot of Instant Pot, place all ingredients and mix.
2. Close the lid and place the pressure valve to "Seal" position.
3. Press "Manual" and cook under "High Pressure" for about 13 minutes.
4. Press "Cancel" and carefully allow a "Quick" release.
5. Open the lid and with tongs, transfer the chicken thighs into a bowl.
6. With 2 forks, shred the chicken.
7. Return chicken into the pot and stir to combine.
8. Serve immediately.

Nutrition:

- Info Per serving:Calories: 322, Fats: 8.2g, Carbs: 25.1g, Sugar: 1.2g, Proteins: 35g, Sodium: 321mg

Sausage And Cauliflower "grits"

Servings: 4

Cooking Time: 20 Minutes

Ingredients:

- 1 pound frozen (uncooked) Italian-style chicken or turkey sausages
- 1 pound frozen riced cauliflower, broken up
- 1 tablespoon extra-virgin olive oil
- Freshly ground black pepper
- ⅓ cup shredded Parmesan cheese
- Chopped fresh parsley, for garnish

Directions:

1. Pour ½ cup of water into the electric pressure cooker and add the sausages.
2. Close and lock the lid of the pressure cooker. Set the valve to sealing.
3. Cook on high pressure for 15 minutes.
4. When the cooking is complete, hit Cancel and quick release the pressure.
5. Once the pin drops, unlock and remove the lid.
6. Using tongs, transfer the sausages to a cutting board and slice into 1-inch rounds. Pour the liquid from the pot into a measuring cup. Pour ½ cup of the liquid back into the pot; discard the rest.
7. In the electric pressure cooker, combine the sliced sausage, cauliflower, olive oil, and pepper. Close and lock the lid of the pressure cooker. Set the valve to sealing.
8. Cook on high pressure for 5 minutes.
9. When the cooking is complete, hit Cancel and quick release the pressure.
10. Once the pin drops, unlock and remove the lid.
11. Stir in the Parmesan, garnish with parsley, and serve immediately.

Nutrition:

- Info Per serving: Calories: 263; Total Fat: 11g; Protein: 30g; Carbohydrates: 11g; Sugars: 4g; Fiber: 3g; Sodium: 660mg

Instant Pot Chicken Breast

Servings: 8

Cooking Time: 20 Minutes

Ingredients:

- 3 lbs. boneless and skinless chicken breasts
- 1 cup water
- 2 tsp. garlic powder
- Black pepper
- 1 tsp. salt

Directions:

1. Pour in water into the Instant Pot and place a trivet with handles inside.
2. Place the chicken breasts into the Instant Pot, arranging them in a single layer.
3. If using frozen chicken make sure each breast is separated, and not touching each other.
4. Season with garlic powder, black pepper, and salt, toss well to mix using tongs or your hands.
5. Close and seal the lid, setting the pressure release vent to "Sealing" and choose the "Manual, High Pressure" setting.
6. Cook for 20 minutes if using fresh chicken or 25 minutes if using frozen chicken breasts.
7. The Instant Pot will take 10 minutes to come to pressure, so factor this time in your cooking.
8. After the cook cycle is done, the Instant Pot will beep, and will need about 20 minutes to come down to pressure. This is known as a Natural Pressure Release, and should take about 10-15 minutes.
9. A quick release will not work for this recipe, as it makes the meat tough.
10. Carefully open the lid and use the chicken breasts for meal prep, casseroles, salads etc.
11. Shred or cube the chicken, and save the stock for other recipes like soup.

Nutrition:

- InfoCalories 204, Carbs 0 g, Fat 4.5 g, Protein 38.3 g, Potassium (K) 496 mg, Sodium (Na) 294.5 mg

Moroccan Chicken Bowls

Servings: 6
Cooking Time: 25 Minutes

Ingredients:
- For the Sweet Potatoes:
- 2 cubed sweet potatoes
- ½ tbsp. olive oil
- 1 tsp. garlic powder
- ½ tbsp. chili powder
- For the chicken:
- 3 tbsp. olive oil
- 1½ lbs. chicken thighs
- 1 chopped white onion
- ⅓ cup raisins
- ½ cup chopped green olives
- ½ cup chicken broth
- 1 tbsp. ground cuminutes
- ½ tbsp. chili powder
- 1 tsp. ginger powder
- 1 tsp. turmeric
- 1½ tsp. garlic powder
- ½ tsp. cayenne
- ⅛ tsp. salt
- For the Couscous:
- 1 cup water
- 1 cup couscous
- Zest of 1 lemon
- 2 tbsp. lemon juice
- ¼ cup chopped cilantro
- ¼ cup chopped parsley
- To Serve:
- Feta cheese
- Pistachios

Directions:

1. Preheat the oven to 400F.
2. Prepare a baking sheet and then put the sweet potatoes onto the baking sheet.
3. Drizzle the potatoes with olive oil, chili powder, and garlic powder, and mix.
4. Bake for 20-25 minutes.
5. Prepare the marinade for the chicken by mixing together the turmeric, cumin, ginger, chili powder, garlic powder, cayenne, and salt.
6. Place the chicken thighs into a bowl and pour over the spices. Rub, making sure each thigh is well coated, and set aside.
7. Select the "Sauté" function on the Instant Pot and then add two tablespoons of olive oil.
8. Once hot, place the chicken thighs with the skin side facing down, and cook for 2-3 minutes.
9. Flip over and cook for 2-3 minutes more, before removing from the Instant Pot.
10. Add all the remaining ingredients for the chicken to the pot, place the chicken on top, and then close and seal your Instant Pot.
11. Set the Instant Pot on the "Manual, High Pressure" setting and once the pot is up to pressure, cook for 25 minutes.
12. As the chicken cooks, prepare the couscous.
13. Bring 2 cups of water to a boil.
14. Place the couscous in a bowl, and add the boiling water to it.
15. Cover with cling wrap, and let rest for 5 minutes. After 5 minutes, uncover the couscous and fluff with a fork.
16. In another large mixing bowl, combine the ingredients for the couscous, and set them aside.
17. When the chicken is done, the naturally release the pressure, about 5-10 minutes.
18. Carefully uncover and remove the chicken from Instant pot and then shred into bits.
19. Discard the skin and bones and return the shredded chicken to the Instant Pot, and mix well with the cooking juices.
20. Serve the chicken with sweet potatoes and couscous, and if desired, top with feta cheese and pistachios.

Nutrition:

- InfoCalories 346, Carbs 30g, Fat 15 g, Protein 26 g, Potassium (K) 941.9 mg, Sodium (Na) 239.9 mg

Thai Green Turkey Curry

Servings: 2
Cooking Time: 20 Minutes

Ingredients:
- 0.5lb chopped cooked turkey
- 0.5 cup minced scallions and greens
- 0.5 cup chopped tomato
- 3tbsp Thai green curry paste
- 1tbsp oil or ghee

Directions:
1. Set the Instant Pot to saute and add the oil and curry paste.
2. When mixed, add the remaining ingredients and seal.
3. Cook on Stew for 20 minutes.
4. Release the pressure naturally.

Nutrition:
- Info Per serving:Calories: 350;Carbs: 16 ;Sugar: 5 ;Fat: 15 ;Protein: 43 ;GL: 12

Chicken Coconut Curry

Servings: 2
Cooking Time: 20 Minutes

Ingredients:

- 0.5lb chopped cooked chicken breast
- 1 thinly sliced onion
- 1 cup coconut milk
- 3tbsp curry paste
- 1tbsp oil or ghee

Directions:

1. Set the Instant Pot to saute and add the onion, oil, and curry paste.
2. When the onion is soft, add the remaining ingredients and seal.
3. Cook on Stew for 20 minutes.
4. Release the pressure naturally.

Nutrition:

- Info Per serving:Calories: 450;Carbs: 27 ;Sugar: 16 ;Fat: 25 ;Protein: 43 ;GL: 21

Chicken Stuffed Potatoes

Servings: 4
Cooking Time: 30 Minutes

Ingredients:

- 6-ounce chicken sausage links
- 4 medium potatoes, each about 8-ounce
- 1 medium zucchini, chopped
- 1 cup chopped green onion
- 1/8 teaspoon salt
- ¼ teaspoon ground black pepper
- ½ teaspoon dried oregano
- 1 teaspoon hot sauce
- 2 tablespoons olive oil, divided
- 2 cups water
- 2 tablespoons crumbled blue cheese, reduced fat

Directions:

1. Plugin instant pot, insert the inner pot, press sauté/simmer button, add 1 tablespoon oil and when hot, add chicken sausage and cook for 3 minutes or until edges are nicely golden brown.
2. Add zucchini and ¾ cup green onion, sprinkle with oregano, pour in 1/3 cup water and cook for 3 minutes or until tender-crisp.
3. Then transfer vegetables from the instant pot to a bowl, drizzle with remaining oil and hot sauce, toss until mixed and keep warm by covering the bowl.
4. Press the cancel button, pour in the remaining water, then insert steamer basket and place potatoes on it.
5. Shut the instant pot with its lid, turn the pressure knob to seal the pot, press the 'manual' button, then press the 'timer' to set the cooking time to 18 minutes and cook at high pressure, instant pot will take 5 minutes or more for building its inner pressure.
6. When the timer beeps, press 'cancel' button and do quick pressure release until pressure nob drops down.
7. Open the instant pot, transfer potatoes to a plate, let cool for 5 minutes, then cut each potato in half.
8. Use fork to fluff potatoes, then season with salt and black pepper and evenly top with prepared sausage and zucchini mixture.
9. Sprinkle remaining green onions and cheese on loaded potatoes and serve straight away.

Nutrition:

- InfoCalories: 350 Cal, Carbs: 45 g, Fat: 12 g, Protein: 16 g, Fiber: 6 g.

BEEF PORK & LAMB RECIPES

Lamb Chops With Beans & Spinach

Servings: 5
Cooking Time: 32 Minutes

Ingredients:

- 4 (6-ounce) bone-in lamb shoulder chops, trimmed
- 1 small onion, chopped finely
- 2 cups hot water
- 2 cups boiled white beans
- 2 cups fresh spinach leaves, torn
- 2 tablespoons olive oil
- Salt and ground black pepper, as required
- 3 garlic cloves, crushed
- 2 tablespoons fresh lemon juice

Directions:

1. In the Instant Pot, place oil and press "Sauté". Now add the leg of lamb and sear for about 2 minutes per side or until browned completely.
2. With a slotted spoon, transfer the chops onto a plate.
3. In the pot, add the onion and garlic and cook for about 1-2 minutes.
4. Press "Cancel" and stir in the hot water, salt and black pepper.
5. Arrange the chops in an even layer and submerge into the liquid.
6. Close the lid and place the pressure valve to "Seal" position.
7. Press "Manual" and cook under "High Pressure" for about 20 minutes.
8. Press "Cancel" and allow a "Natural" release for about 10 minutes. Then allow a "Quick" release.
9. Open the lid and transfer lamb chops into a large bowl.
10. With 2 forks shred the meat.
11. Press "Sauté" and cook for about 3-4 minutes.
12. Stir in the lamb meat and beans and cook for about 1-2 minutes or until desired thickness.
13. Press "Cancel" and stir in the spinach until wilted.
14. Stir in lemon juice and serve hot.

Nutrition:

- Info Per serving:Calories: 361, Fats: 16.6g, Carbs: 19.3g, Sugar: 1.6g, Proteins: 33.5g, Sodium: 181mg

Fabada

Servings: 2
Cooking Time: 5 Minutes

Ingredients:
- 0.5lb cubed ham
- 0.5lb black pudding
- 1lb cooked beans
- 1 cup low sodium broth
- 1tbsp spicy seasoning

Directions:
1. Mix all the ingredients in your Instant Pot.
2. Cook on Stew for 5 minutes. Release the pressure naturally.

Nutrition:
- Info Per serving:Calories: 300;Carbs: 20 ;Sugar: 2 ;Fat: 15 ;Protein: 35 ;GL: 9

Veal In Milk

Servings: 2
Cooking Time: 35 Minutes

Ingredients:
- 1lb veal steak
- 1lb chopped vegetables
- 2 cups whole milk
- 1tbsp black pepper seasoning mix

Directions:
1. Mix all the ingredients in your Instant Pot.
2. Cook on Stew for 35 minutes.
3. Release the pressure naturally.

Nutrition:
- Info Per serving:Calories: 270;Carbs: 2 ;Sugar: 0 ;Fat: 16 ;Protein: 39 ;GL: 1

Oxtail Soup

Servings: 2

Cooking Time: 35 Minutes

Ingredients:

- 1lb of prepared ox tail
- 1lb chopped Mediterranean vegetables
- 1 cup low sodium beef broth

Directions:

1. Mix all the ingredients in your Instant Pot.
2. Cook on Stew for 35 minutes.
3. Release the pressure naturally.

Nutrition:

- Info Per serving:Calories: 200;Carbs: 2 ;Sugar: 0 ;Fat: 6 ;Protein: 37 ;GL: 1

Beef Goulash

Servings: 8
Cooking Time: 45 Minutes

Ingredients:
- 2 pounds beef roast, cut into 1-inch cubes
- 6 medium carrots, peeled and cut into 1-inch pieces
- 1 medium white onion, peeled and cut into 1-inch pieces
- 2 teaspoon salt
- 1/4 cup cornstarch
- 2 tablespoons onion soup mix
- 2 teaspoons paprika
- 2 teaspoons Worcestershire sauce
- 2 cups beef broth
- 2 tablespoon olive oil
- 1/3 cup water

Directions:
1. Cut beef into 1-inch cubes and season with salt.
2. Plugin instant pot, insert the inner pot, press sauté/simmer button, add oil and when hot, add seasoned beef pieces in a single layer and cook for 4 minutes per side or until nicely browned.
3. Cook remaining beef pieces in the same manner, then transfer into a bowl, add onions into the pot and cook for 5 minutes or until sauté.
4. Add carrots, season with paprika and onion soup mix, drizzle with Worcestershire sauce and pour in beef broth.
5. Return beef pieces into the instant pot, stir until just mixed and press the cancel button.
6. Shut the instant pot with its lid, turn the pressure knob to seal the pot, press the 'meat/stew' button, then press the 'timer' to set the cooking time to 20 minutes and cook at high pressure, instant pot will take 5 minutes or more for building its inner pressure.
7. When the timer beeps, press 'cancel' button and do natural pressure release for 10 minutes and then do quick pressure release until pressure nob drops down.
8. Open the instant pot, stir the stew and press the 'sauté/simmer' button.
9. Stir together cornstarch and water until combined, add to the instant pot, stir well and cook for 3 minutes or more until cooking sauce is thick to the desired level.
10. Serve straight away.

Nutrition:
- InfoCalories: 315 Cal, Carbs: 17 g, Fat: 17 g, Protein: 24 g, Fiber: 2 g.

Fruity Pork Loin

Servings: 4
Cooking Time: 40 Minutes

Ingredients:

- 1 1/3 pounds boneless pork tenderloin
- 2 cups apples, cored and chopped
- 2/3 cup fresh cherries, pitted
- ½ cup onion, chopped
- ½ cup fresh apple juice
- Salt and ground black pepper, as required

Directions:

1. In the pot of Instant Pot, place all ingredients and stir to combine.
2. Close the lid and place the pressure valve to "Seal" position.
3. Press "Meat" and just use the default time of 40 minutes.
4. Press "Cancel" and carefully allow a "Quick" release.
5. Open the lid and transfer the pork onto a cutting board.
6. Cut into desired sized pieces and serve alongside apple mixture.

Nutrition:

- Info Per serving:Calories: 255, Fats: 4.3g, Carbs: 25,3g, Sugar: 19g, Proteins: 29.2g, Sodium: 339mg

5-ingredient Mexican Lasagna

Servings: 4
Cooking Time: 15 Minutes

Ingredients:
- Nonstick cooking spray
- ½ (15-ounce) can light red kidney beans, rinsed and drained
- 4 (6-inch) gluten-free corn tortillas
- 1½ cups cooked shredded beef, pork, or chicken
- 1⅓ cups salsa
- 1⅓ cups shredded Mexican cheese blend

Directions:
1. Spray a 6-inch springform pan with nonstick spray. Wrap the bottom in foil.
2. In a medium bowl, mash the beans with a fork.
3. Place 1 tortilla in the bottom of the pan. Add about ⅓ of the beans, ½ cup of meat, ⅓ cup of salsa, and ⅓ cup of cheese. Press down. Repeat for 2 more layers. Add the remaining tortilla and press down. Top with the remaining salsa and cheese. There are no beans or meat on the top layer.
4. Tear off a piece of foil big enough to cover the pan, and spray it with nonstick spray. Line the pan with the foil, sprayed-side down.
5. Pour 1 cup of water into the electric pressure cooker.
6. Place the pan on the wire rack and carefully lower it into the pot. Close and lock the lid of the pressure cooker. Set the valve to sealing.
7. Cook on high pressure for 15 minutes.
8. When the cooking is complete, hit Cancel. Allow the pressure to release naturally for 10 minutes, then quick release any remaining pressure.
9. Once the pin drops, unlock and remove the lid.
10. Using the handles of the wire rack, carefully remove the pan from the pot. Let the lasagna sit for 5 minutes. Carefully remove the ring.
11. Slice into quarters and serve.

Nutrition:
- Info Per serving: Calories: 395; Total Fat: 16g; Protein: 30g; Carbohydrates: 34g; Sugars: 5g; Fiber: 9g; Sodium: 1140mg

FISH AND SEAFOOD RECIPES

Rosemary Salmon

Servings: 3
Cooking Time: 15 Minutes

Ingredients:

- 1 tbsp. olive oil
- 1 lb. frozen, wild-caught salmon
- 1 sprig fresh rosemary
- 10 oz. fresh asparagus
- ½ cup halved cherry tomatoes
- 1 tbsp. lemon juice
- 1 tsp. Kosher salt
- Black pepper

Directions:

1. Pour a cup of water into the Instant Pot and place a wire rack into the pot.
2. Place the fish in a single layer onto the rack, and then add a sprig of rosemary and finally the fresh asparagus.
3. Choose the "Manual, High pressure" setting and adjust the cook time to 3 minutes.
4. Once done, release the pressure and uncover the pot.
5. Remove the lid and transfer all the contents onto a plate, discarding the rosemary.
6. Add the cherry tomatoes, drizzle with olive oil and season with salt and black pepper.
7. Sprinkle with lemon juice and serve.

Nutrition:

- InfoCalories 282, Carbs 5g, Fat 14 g, Protein 32 g, Potassium (K) 985 mg, Sodium (Na) 71 mg

Swordfish Steak

Servings: 2
Cooking Time: 35 Minutes

Ingredients:
- 1lb swordfish steak, whole
- 1lb chopped Mediterranean vegetables
- 1 cup low sodium fish broth
- 2tbsp soy sauce

Directions:
1. Mix all the ingredients except the broth in a foil pouch.
2. Place the pouch in the steamer basket for your Instant Pot.
3. Pour the broth into the Instant Pot. Lower the steamer basket into the Instant Pot.
4. Cook on Steam for 35 minutes.
5. Release the pressure naturally.

Nutrition:
- Info Per serving:Calories: 270;Carbs: 5 ;Sugar: 1 ;Fat: 10 ;Protein: 48 ;GL: 1

Shrimp With Tomatoes And Feta

Servings: 6

Cooking Time: 12 Minutes

Ingredients:
- 2 tbsp. butter
- 1 lb. frozen shrimp
- 1 tbsp. garlic
- 1½ cups chopped white onion
- 14.5 oz. crushed tomatoes
- 1 tsp. dried oregano
- 1 tsp. sea salt
- ½ tsp. red pepper flakes, or to taste
- To Serve:
- 1 cup crumbled feta cheese
- ½ cup sliced black olives
- ¼ cup fresh parsley

Directions:
1. Select the "Sauté" function on your Instant Pot and once hot, add the butter.
2. Melt the butter and then add the garlic and red pepper flakes.
3. Next, add in the onions, tomatoes, salt, and oregano.
4. Add the frozen shrimp.
5. Set the Instant pot on "Manual, High Pressure" setting for1 minute.
6. Once done, release all the pressure and stir well to combine all the ingredients.
7. Allow to cool and then sprinkle with feta cheese, black olives, and parsley.
8. Serve with buttered French bread, or rice.

Nutrition:
- InfoCalories 211, Carbs 6g, Fat 11 g, Protein 19 g, Potassium (K) 148 mg, Sodium (Na) 1468 mg

Sardine Curry

Servings: 2
Cooking Time: 35 Minutes

Ingredients:
- 5 tins of sardines in tomato
- 1lb chopped vegetables
- 1 cup low sodium fish broth
- 3tbsp curry paste

Directions:
1. Mix all the ingredients in your Instant Pot.
2. Cook on Stew for 35 minutes.
3. Release the pressure naturally.

Nutrition:
- Info Per serving:Calories: 320;Carbs: 8 ;Sugar: 2 ;Fat: 16 ;Protein: 42 ;GL: 3

Shrimp Coconut Curry

Servings: 2
Cooking Time: 20 Minutes

Ingredients:
- 0.5lb cooked shrimp
- 1 thinly sliced onion
- 1 cup coconut yogurt
- 3tbsp curry paste
- 1tbsp oil or ghee

Directions:
1. Set the Instant Pot to saute and add the onion, oil, and curry paste.
2. When the onion is soft, add the remaining ingredients and seal.
3. Cook on Stew for 20 minutes.
4. Release the pressure naturally.

Nutrition:
- Info Per serving:Calories: 380;Carbs: 13 ;Sugar: 4 ;Fat: 22 ;Protein: 40 ;GL: 14

Sweet & Sour Tuna

Servings: 4
Cooking Time: 9 Minutes

Ingredients:

- 4 (6-ounce) tuna steaks, pat dried
- ½ cup low-sodium chicken broth
- 2 tablespoon Yacon syrup
- 2 tablespoon balsamic vinegar
- 2 tablespoons kaffir lime leaves, minced
- 1 (½-inch) piece fresh ginger, minced
- Ground black pepper, as required

Directions:

1. In the pot of Instant pot, place all the ingredients and mix well.
2. Add the tuna steaks and mix with broth mixture.
3. Secure the lid and place the pressure valve to "Seal" position
4. Press "Manual" and cook under "High Pressure" for about 6 minutes.
5. Press "Cancel" and carefully allow a "Quick" release.
6. Open the lid and with a slotted spoon, transfer the tuna steaks onto a plate.
7. Press "Sauté" and cook for about 2-3 minutes or until sauce becomes slightly thick.
8. Press "Cancel" and pour the sauce over tuna steaks.
9. Serve immediately.

Nutrition:

- Info Per serving:Calories: 329, Fats: 10.7g, Carbs: 3.3g, Sugar: 1.8g, Proteins: 5.1g, Sodium: 97mg

Coconut Shrimp Curry

Servings: 4
Cooking Time: 15 Minutes

Ingredients:

- 1 tbsp. vegetable oil
- 1 lb. frozen shrimp
- 1 cup chopped white onion
- ½ tbsp. minced ginger
- ½ tbsp. minced garlic
- 1 tsp. mustard seeds
- 1 green chili pepper
- 1 cup chopped tomato
- ¼ can coconut milk
- 1 tbsp. lime juice
- ¼ cup cilantro
- For the Spice mix:
- 1 tsp. coriander powder
- ½ tsp. cayenne or red chili powder
- ½ tsp. ground turmeric
- ½ tsp. garam masala
- ½ tsp. sea salt

Directions:

1. Select the "Sauté" function on the instant Pot and allow it to heat up.
2. Add the oil and mustard seeds and sizzle them until they begin to pop.
3. Add the onions, ginger, garlic and green chili.
4. Sauté for 5 minutes until the onions are a light golden brown and the garlic and ginger aromatic.
5. Add the tomato and all the spices. Mix and sauté for 2-3 minutes.
6. Now, add the coconut milk and shrimp. Stir and select the "Cancel" button. Close the lid with steam release vent in the "Sealing" position.
7. Cook on the "Manual, Low Pressure" setting for 3 minutes.
8. Once done, quick release the pressure manually.
9. Stir in the lime and garnish with cilantro.
10. Enjoy and serve with rice.

Nutrition:

- InfoCalories 226, Carbs 8g, Fat 10 g, Protein 24 g, Potassium (K) 289 mg, Sodium (Na) 1222 mg

Salmon In Green Sauce

Servings: 4

Cooking Time: 12 Minutes

Ingredients:

- 4 (6-ounce) salmon fillets
- 1 avocado, peeled, pitted and chopped
- ½ cup fresh basil, chopped
- 3 garlic cloves, chopped
- 1 tablespoon fresh lemon zest, grated finely

Directions:

1. Grease a large piece of foil.
2. In a large bowl, add all ingredients except salmon and water and with a fork, mash completely.
3. Place fillets in the center of foil and top with avocado mixture evenly.
4. Fold the foil around fillets to seal them.
5. Arrange a steamer trivet in the Instant Pot and pour ½ cup of water.
6. Place the foil packet on top of trivet.
7. Close the lid and place the pressure valve to "Seal" position.
8. Press "Manual" and cook under "High Pressure" for about 8 minutes.
9. Meanwhile, preheat the oven to broiler.
10. Press "Cancel" and allow a "Natural" release.
11. Open the lid and transfer the salmon fillets onto a broiler pan.
12. Broil for about 3-4 minutes.
13. Serve warm.

Nutrition:

- Info Per serving:Calories: 333, Fats: 20.3g, Carbs: 5.5g, Sugar: 0.4g, Proteins: 34.2g, Sodium: 79mg

VEGAN AND VEGETABLE RECIPES

Squash Medley

Servings: 2
Cooking Time: 20 Minutes.

Ingredients:
- 2lbs mixed squash
- 0.5 cup mixed veg
- 1 cup vegetable stock
- 2tbsp olive oil
- 2tbsp mixed herbs

Directions:
1. Put the squash in the steamer basket and add the stock into the Instant Pot.
2. Steam the squash in your Instant Pot for 10 minutes.
3. Depressurize and pour away the remaining stock.
4. Set to saute and add the oil and remaining ingredients.
5. Cook until a light crust forms.

Nutrition:
- Info Per serving:Calories: 100;Carbs: 10 ;Sugar: 3 ;Fat: 6 ;Protein: 5 ;GL: 20

Split Pea Stew

Servings: 2
Cooking Time: 35 Minutes

Ingredients:
- 1 cup dry split peas
- 1 lb. chopped vegetables
- 1 cup mushroom soup
- 2 tbsps. old bay seasoning

Directions:
1. Mix all the ingredients in your Instant Pot, cook on Beans for 35 minutes.
2. Release the pressure naturally.

Nutrition:
- InfoCalories 300, Carbs 7g, Fat 2g, Protein 24g, Potassium (K) 63.2 mg, Sodium (Na) 797.7 mg

Eggplant Curry

Servings: 2

Cooking Time: 20 Minutes

Ingredients:
- 2-3 cups chopped eggplant
- 1 thinly sliced onion
- 1 cup coconut milk
- 3tbsp curry paste
- 1tbsp oil or ghee

Directions:
1. Set the Instant Pot to saute and add the onion, oil, and curry paste.
2. When the onion is soft, add the remaining ingredients and seal.
3. Cook on Stew for 20 minutes. Release the pressure naturally.

Nutrition:
- Info Per serving:Calories: 350;Carbs: 15 ;Sugar: 3 ;Fat: 25 ;Protein: 11 ;GL: 10

Seitan Roast

Servings: 2
Cooking Time: 35 Minutes

Ingredients:
- 1lb seitan roulade
- 1lb chopped winter vegetables
- 1 cup low sodium vegetable broth
- 4tbsp roast rub

Directions:
1. Rub the roast rub into your roulade.
2. Place the roulade and vegetables in your Instant Pot.
3. Add the broth. Seal.
4. Cook on Stew for 35 minutes.
5. Release the pressure naturally.

Nutrition:
- Info Per serving:Calories: 260;Carbs: 9 ;Sugar: 2 ;Fat: 2 ;Protein: 49 ;GL: 4

Chili Sin Carne

Servings: 2

Cooking Time: 35 Minutes

Ingredients:

- 3 cups mixed cooked beans
- 2 cups chopped tomatoes
- 1tbsp yeast extract
- 2 squares very dark chocolate
- 1tbsp red chili flakes

Directions:

1. Mix all the ingredients in your Instant Pot.
2. Cook on Beans for 35 minutes.
3. Release the pressure naturally.

Nutrition:

- Info Per serving:Calories: 240;Carbs: 20 ;Sugar: 5 ;Fat: 3 ;Protein: 36 ;GL: 11

Lentil And Eggplant Stew

Servings: 2
Cooking Time: 35 Minutes

Ingredients:
- 1lb eggplant
- 1lb dry lentils
- 1 cup chopped vegetables
- 1 cup low sodium vegetable broth

Directions:
1. Mix all the ingredients in your Instant Pot.
2. Cook on Stew for 35 minutes.
3. Release the pressure naturally.

Nutrition:
- Info Per serving:Calories: 310;Carbs: 22 ;Sugar: 6 ;Fat: 10 ;Protein: 32 ;GL: 16

Seitan Curry

Servings: 2
Cooking Time: 20 Minutes

Ingredients:
- 0.5lb seitan
- 1 thinly sliced onion
- 1 cup chopped tomato
- 3tbsp curry paste
- 1tbsp oil or ghee

Directions:
1. Set the Instant Pot to saute and add the onion, oil, and curry paste.
2. When the onion is soft, add the remaining ingredients and seal.
3. Cook on Stew for 20 minutes.
4. Release the pressure naturally.

Nutrition:
- Info Per serving:Calories: 240;Carbs: 19 ;Sugar: 4 ;Fat: 10 ;Protein: 32 ;GL: 10

Mango Tofu Curry

Servings: 2
Cooking Time: 35 Minutes

Ingredients:
- 1lb cubed extra firm tofu
- 1lb chopped vegetables
- 1 cup low carb mango sauce
- 1 cup vegetable broth
- 2tbsp curry paste

Directions:
1. Mix all the ingredients in your Instant Pot.
2. Cook on Stew for 35 minutes.
3. Release the pressure naturally.

Nutrition:
- Info Per serving:Calories: 310;Carbs: 20 ;Sugar: 9 ;Fat: 4 ;Protein: 37 ;GL: 19

SOUPS & STEWS RECIPES

Kidney Bean Stew

Servings: 2
Cooking Time: 15 Minutes

Ingredients:
- 1lb cooked kidney beans
- 1 cup tomato passata
- 1 cup low sodium beef broth
- 3tbsp Italian herbs

Directions:
1. Mix all the ingredients in your Instant Pot.
2. Cook on Stew for 15 minutes.
3. Release the pressure naturally.

Nutrition:
- Info Per serving:Calories: 270;Carbs: 16 ;Sugar: 3 ;Fat: 10 ;Protein: 23 ;GL: 8

Sweet And Sour Soup

Servings: 2
Cooking Time: 35 Minutes

Ingredients:
- 1lb cubed chicken breast
- 1lb chopped vegetables
- 1 cup low carb sweet and sour sauce
- 0.5 cup diabetic marmalade

Directions:
1. Mix all the ingredients in your Instant Pot.
2. Cook on Stew for 35 minutes.
3. Release the pressure naturally.

Nutrition:
- Info Per serving:Calories: 270;Carbs: 22 ;Sugar: 9 ;Fat: 2 ;Protein: 36 ;GL: 12

Egg Salad

Servings: 4
Cooking Time: 5 Minutes

Ingredients:

- 8 eggs
- ¼ cup celery, diced
- ⅓ cup homemade mayonnaise
- 1 tsp. sea salt
- ½ tsp. black pepper
- Cooking oil spray

Directions:

1. Lightly spray a baking or casserole dish with cooking oil spray and crack the eggs into the dish.
2. Place a wire steamer rack in the bottom of the Instant Pot and add a cup of water.
3. Place the baking dish on the rack and seal the Instant Pot lid.
4. Cook on the "Manual, High Pressure" setting for 5 minutes, and then release the steam manually when the cook cycle completes.
5. Remove the baking dish from the pot and slide the egg loaf onto a cutting board.
6. Chop and then combine with mayonnaise, celery, salt, and black pepper.
7. Chill until ready to serve.

Nutrition:

- InfoCalories 266, Carbs 5.3g, Fat 22g, Protein 11g, Potassium (K) 137 mg, Sodium (Na) 714 mg

Chili Con Carne

Servings: 2
Cooking Time: 35 Minutes

Ingredients:
- 1lb minced beef
- 1 cup mixed beans
- 2 cups chopped tomatoes
- 3 squares very dark chocolate
- 3tbsp mixed seasoning

Directions:
1. Mix all the ingredients in your Instant Pot.
2. Cook on Stew for 35 minutes.
3. Release the pressure naturally.

Nutrition:
- Info Per serving:Calories: 340;Carbs: 16 ;Sugar: 6 ;Fat: 12 ;Protein: 46 ;GL: 14

Zucchini Soup

Servings: 2
Cooking Time: 12 Minutes

Ingredients:

- 2 medium zucchinis, chopped
- 1/2 teaspoon onion powder
- 1/2 teaspoon garlic powder
- 1/2 teaspoon salt
- 1/4 teaspoon ground black pepper
- 1/2 teaspoon curry powder
- 1 cup coconut milk, reduced-fat and unsweetened
- 1 cup of water

Directions:

1. Plugin instant pot, insert the inner pot, pour in water, then insert steamer basket and place zucchini pies on it.
2. Shut the instant pot with its lid and turn the pressure knob to seal the pot.
3. Press the 'steam' button, then press the 'timer' to set the cooking time to 2 minutes and cook at high pressure, instant pot will take 5 minutes or more for building its inner pressure.
4. When the timer beeps, press 'cancel' button and do natural pressure release for 5 minutes and then do quick pressure release until pressure nob drops down.
5. Open the instant pot, transfer zucchini to a plate to cool for 5 minutes, then place zucchini pieces in a food processor and add remaining ingredients.
6. Pulse zucchini for 1 to 2 minutes or until smooth and then evenly divide between bowls.
7. Serve straight away.

Nutrition:

- InfoCalories: 141 Cal, Carbs: 7 g, Fat: 11 g, Protein: 3.5 g, Fiber: 3 g.

Irish Beef Stew

Servings: 4
Cooking Time: 35 Minutes

Ingredients:
- 1-pound beef, cut into 1-inch pieces
- 1 large white onion, peeled and diced
- 2 stalks of celery, sliced
- 2 medium potatoes, cut into 1-inch pieces
- 2 medium carrots, peeled and sliced
- 1 teaspoon minced garlic
- 1 teaspoon salt
- 1/2 teaspoon ground black pepper
- 1 teaspoon dried thyme
- 1 tablespoon dried parsley
- 1 bay leaf
- 1 tablespoon olive oil
- 1 cup beef stock
- 2 tablespoons cornstarch
- 2 tablespoons warm water

Directions:
1. Plugin instant pot, insert the inner pot, press sauté/simmer button, add oil and when hot, add onion, celery, carrot, and garlic and cook for 5 minutes or until softened.
2. Add remaining ingredients, except for cornstarch and warm water, stir until mixed and press the cancel button.
3. Shut the instant pot with its lid, turn the pressure knob to seal the pot, press the 'manual' button, then press the 'timer' to set the cooking time to 20 minutes and cook at high pressure, instant pot will take 5 minutes or more for building its inner pressure.
4. When the timer beeps, press 'cancel' button and do natural pressure release for 10 minutes and then do quick pressure release until pressure nob drops down.
5. Open the instant pot, stir together cornstarch and water, add into the stew, stir well and let stew rest for 5 minutes or until slightly thick.
6. Ladle stew into the bowls and serve.

Nutrition:
- InfoCalories: 392.8 Cal, Carbs: 61.6 g, Fat: 4.1 g, Protein: 29.1 g, Fiber: 9.8 g.

Spicy Pepper Soup

Servings: 2
Cooking Time: 15 Minutes

Ingredients:
- 1lb chopped mixed sweet peppers
- 1 cup low sodium vegetable broth
- 3tbsp chopped chili peppers
- 1tbsp black pepper

Directions:
1. Mix all the ingredients in your Instant Pot.
2. Cook on Stew for 15 minutes.
3. Release the pressure naturally. Blend.

Nutrition:
- Info Per serving:Calories: 100;Carbs: 11 ;Sugar: 4 ;Fat: 2 ;Protein: 3 ;GL: 6

Broccoli Stilton Soup

Servings: 2
Cooking Time: 35 Minutes

Ingredients:
- 1lb chopped broccoli
- 0.5lb chopped vegetables
- 1 cup low sodium vegetable broth
- 1 cup Stilton

Directions:
1. Mix all the ingredients in your Instant Pot.
2. Cook on Stew for 35 minutes.
3. Release the pressure naturally.
4. Blend the soup.

Nutrition:
- Info Per serving:Calories: 280;Carbs: 9 ;Sugar: 2 ;Fat: 22 ;Protein: 13 ;GL: 4

DESSERTS RECIPES

Spiced Pear Applesauce

Servings: 3½ Cups
Cooking Time: 5 Minutes

Ingredients:

- 2 pounds apples, peeled, cored, and sliced
- 1 pound pears, peeled, cored, and sliced
- 2 teaspoons apple pie spice or cinnamon
- Pinch kosher salt
- Juice of ½ small lemon

Directions:

1. In the electric pressure cooker, combine the apples, pears, apple pie spice, salt, lemon juice, and ¼ cup of water.
2. Close and lock the lid of the pressure cooker. Set the valve to sealing.
3. Cook on high pressure for 5 minutes.
4. When the cooking is complete, hit Cancel and let the pressure release naturally.
5. Once the pin drops, unlock and remove the lid.
6. Mash the apples and pears with a potato masher to the consistency you like.
7. Serve warm, or cool to room temperature and refrigerate.

Nutrition:

- Info Per serving(½ CUP): Calories: 108; Total Fat: 1g; Protein: 1g; Carbohydrates: 29g; Sugars: 20g; Fiber: 6g; Sodium: 15mg

Crustless Key Lime Cheesecake

Servings: 8
Cooking Time: 35 Minutes

Ingredients:

- Nonstick cooking spray
- 16 ounces light cream cheese (Neufchâtel), softened
- ⅔ cup granulated erythritol sweetener
- ¼ cup unsweetened Key lime juice (I like Nellie & Joe's Famous Key West Lime Juice)
- ½ teaspoon vanilla extract
- ¼ cup plain Greek yogurt
- 1 teaspoon grated lime zest
- 2 large eggs
- Whipped cream, for garnish (optional)

Directions:

1. Spray a 7-inch springform pan with nonstick cooking spray. Line the bottom and partway up the sides of the pan with foil.
2. Put the cream cheese in a large bowl. Use an electric mixer to whip the cream cheese until smooth, about 2 minutes. Add the erythritol, lime juice, vanilla, yogurt, and zest, and blend until smooth. Stop the mixer and scrape down the sides of the bowl with a rubber spatula. With the mixer on low speed, add the eggs, one at a time, blending until just mixed. (Don't overbeat the eggs.)
3. Pour the mixture into the prepared pan. Drape a paper towel over the top of the pan, not touching the cream cheese mixture, and tightly wrap the top of the pan in foil. (Your goal here is to keep out as much moisture as possible.)
4. Pour 1 cup of water into the electric pressure cooker.
5. Place the foil-covered pan onto the wire rack and carefully lower it into the pot.
6. Close and lock the lid of the pressure cooker. Set the valve to sealing.
7. Cook on high pressure for 35 minutes.
8. When the cooking is complete, hit Cancel. Allow the pressure to release naturally for 20 minutes, then quick release any remaining pressure.
9. Once the pin drops, unlock and remove the lid.
10. Using the handles of the wire rack, carefully transfer the pan to a cooling rack. Cool to room temperature, then refrigerate for at least 3 hours.
11. When ready to serve, run a thin rubber spatula around the rim of the cheesecake to loosen it, then remove the ring.
12. Slice into wedges and serve with whipped cream (if using).

Nutrition:

- Info Per serving(1 SLICE): Calories: 157; Total Fat: 12g; Protein: 8g; Carbohydrates: 4g; Sugars: 1g; Fiber: 0g; Sodium: 196mg

Brownies

Servings: 16
Cooking Time: 55 Minutes

Ingredients:

- 3/4 cup whole wheat flour
- 1/2 teaspoon salt
- 1/2 teaspoon baking powder
- 1/2 cup cocoa powder, unsweetened
- 1 cup swerve sweetener
- 1 cup chocolate chips, unsweetened
- 1 teaspoon vanilla extract, unsweetened
- 1/2 cup butter, soften
- 2 eggs
- 1 ½ cup water

Directions:

1. Place butter in a bowl, cream with a beater, then beat in sweetener until combined and beat in eggs and vanilla until incorporated.
2. Place flour in a bowl, add salt, baking powder, cocoa powder and stir until combined.
3. Stir the flour mixture into the egg mixture, 2 tablespoons at a time, until incorporated and then fold in chocolate chips until combined.
4. Take a 7 by 3 push pan or pan that fits into the instant pot, grease it with oil, then spoon in prepared batter, smooth the top and cover with aluminum foil.
5. Plugin instant pot, insert the inner pot, pour in water, insert trivet stand and place brownie pan on it.
6. Shut the instant pot with its lid, turn the pressure knob to seal the pot, press the 'manual' button, then press the 'timer' to set the cooking time to 50 minutes and cook at high pressure, instant pot will take 5 minutes or more for building its inner pressure.
7. When the timer beeps, press 'cancel' button and do natural pressure release for 10 minutes and then do quick pressure release until pressure nob drops down.
8. Open the instant pot, remove the pan, uncover it and let brownies cool in pan on wire rack.
9. Cut brownies into squares and serve.

Nutrition:

- InfoCalories: 200 Cal, Carbs: 24 g, Fat: 11 g, Protein: 2 g, Fiber: 1 g.

Egg Custard

Servings: 4

Cooking Time: 4 Minutes

Ingredients:

- 1½ cups unsweetened almond milk, divided
- 3 large eggs
- 5 tablespoons Erythritol
- Pinch of salt

Directions:

1. In the pot of Instant Pot, place 1 cup of almond milk, Erythritol and salt and press "Sauté".
2. Cook for about 3-4 minutes or until Erythritol is dissolved completely, stirring continuously.
3. Press "Cancel" and transfer the almond milk mixture into a bowl.
4. Set aside to cool slightly.
5. In the pot, add remaining almond milk and mix well.
6. In a large glass bowl, add eggs and beat well.
7. Slowly pour the almond t milk mixture, beating continuously until well combined.
8. Through a fine mesh strainer, strain the egg mixture twice.
9. Now, place the egg mixture into 4 (3x1½-inch) ramekins evenly.
10. With a spoon, remove any air bubbles.
11. With 1 foil piece, cover each ramekin tightly.
12. Arrange a steamer trivet in the Instant Pot and pour 1 cup of water.
13. Place the ramekins on top of trivet.
14. Close the lid and place the pressure valve to "Seal" position.
15. Press "Manual" and cook under "Low Pressure" for about 0 minute.
16. Press "Cancel" and allow a "Natural" release for about 10 minutes. Then allow a "Quick" release.
17. Open the lid and transfer the ramekins onto a wire rack.
18. Remove the foil pieces and set aside to cool slightly.
19. Serve warm.

Nutrition:

- Info Per serving:Calories: 69, Fats: 6g, Carbs: 1g, Sugar: 0.3g, Proteins: 5.1g, Sodium: 159mg

Chia Pudding With Mango

Servings: 2
Cooking Time: 10 Minutes

Ingredients:
- 1/4 cup chia seeds
- 1 cup orange juice
- 1 cup chopped mango
- 4tbsp sweetener

Directions:
1. Pour the milk into your Instant Pot.
2. Add the remaining ingredients, stir well.
3. Seal and close the vent.
4. Choose Manual and set to cook 10 minutes.
5. Release the pressure naturally.

Nutrition:
- Info Per serving:Calories: 320;Carbs: 12 ;Sugar: 5 ;Fat: 6 ;Protein: 8 ;GL: 7

Vanilla Mug Cake

Servings: 2

Cooking Time: 10 Minutes

Ingredients:

- ¾ cup almond flour 2 eggs 2 tablespoons yacon syrup
- 1 teaspoon organic vanilla extract Pinch of salt

Directions:

1. In a bowl, place all the ingredients and stir to combine.
2. Divide the mixture into 2 (8-ounce) greased mason jars evenly.
3. With a piece of foil, cover each jar.
4. Arrange a steamer trivet in the Instant Pot and pour 1 cup of water.
5. Place the jars on top of trivet.
6. Close the lid and place the pressure valve to "Seal" position.
7. Press "Manual" and cook under "High Pressure" for about 10 minutes.
8. Press "Cancel" and carefully allow a "Quick" release.
9. Open the lid and serve warm.

Nutrition:

- Info Per serving:Calories: 364, Fats: 26.9g, Carbs: 14.1g, Sugar: 5.6g, Proteins: 5.5g, Sodium: 146mg

Oatmeal Bites

Servings: 12
Cooking Time: 15 Minutes

Ingredients:
- 1 cup mixed berries, slightly mashed
- 1 cup rolled oats
- 1/2 cup whole wheat flour
- 1/4 teaspoon salt
- 1 tablespoon brown sugar
- 1/2 teaspoon cinnamon
- 1 teaspoon baking powder
- 1/3 cup honey
- 4 eggs
- 1 cup water

Directions:
1. Place oats and flour in a bowl, add salt, cinnamon and baking powder and stir until mixed.
2. Crack eggs in a bowl, add sugar and honey and beat until well combined.
3. Then fold in flour mixture, 4 tablespoons at a time, until incorporated and then fold in berries.
4. Take twelve egg molds, grease them with oil, and then fill each portion with a scoop of cookie mixture, about 3 tablespoons.
5. Plugin instant pot, insert the inner pot, pour in water, then insert steamer basket and place egg molds on it.
6. Shut the instant pot with its lid, turn the pressure knob to seal the pot, press the 'manual' button, then press the 'timer' to set the cooking time to 10 minutes and cook at high pressure, instant pot will take 5 minutes or more for building its inner pressure.
7. When the timer beeps, press 'cancel' button and do natural pressure release for 10 minutes and then do quick pressure release until pressure nob drops down.
8. Open the instant pot, transfer egg molds to a wire rack to cool oatmeal bites, then take them out and dust with powdered sweetener.
9. Serve straight away.

Nutrition:
- InfoCalories: 36.7 Cal, Carbs: 6.2 g, Fat: 1 g, Protein: 1.2 g, Fiber: 0.7 g.

Apple And Cinnamon Cake

Servings: 8
Cooking Time: 65 Minutes

Ingredients:
- 3 large apples, peeled, cored and diced
- 1/2 tablespoon ground cinnamon
- ¾ cup and 2 tablespoons swerve sweetener
- 1 1/2 cups flour and more as needed
- 1/2 tablespoon baking powder
- 1/2 teaspoon salt
- 1/2 cup olive oil
- 1 teaspoon vanilla extract, unsweetened
- 2 eggs
- 1 cup water

Directions:
1. Place diced apples in a bowl, add cinnamon and 2 tablespoons sweetener and toss until evenly coated, set aside until required.
2. Place flour in a large bowl, add salt and baking powder and stir until mixed.
3. Crack eggs in another bowl, add vanilla, oil and remaining sugar and beat until well combined.
4. Then stir in flour mixture, 4 tablespoons at a time, until incorporated and then pour half of this mixture into a greased 7-inch cake pan.
5. Spread half of the apples on the batter in a cake pan, then pour remaining batter on the apple pieces and scatter remaining apples on top along with any juices.
6. Plugin instant pot, insert the inner pot, pour in water, and insert a steamer basket.
7. Cover cake pan with aluminum foil, then place it on the steamer basket, shut the instant pot with its lid and turn the pressure knob to seal the pot.
8. Press the 'manual' button, then press the 'timer' to set the cooking time to 60 minutes and cook at high pressure, instant pot will take 5 minutes or more for building its inner pressure.
9. When the timer beeps, press 'cancel' button and do quick pressure release until pressure nob drops down.
10. Open the instant pot, take out the cake pan, uncover it, and let the cake cool on wire rack.
11. Slice the cake and serve.

Nutrition:
- InfoCalories: 275 Cal, Carbs: 35 g, Fat: 14 g, Protein: 2 g, Fiber: 1 g.

APPETIZERS AND SNACKS

Candied Walnuts

Servings: 20
Cooking Time: 15 Minutes

Ingredients:

- 4 cups raw walnuts
- ¼ cup Yacon syrup
- ½ cup water
- 1 teaspoon olive oil
- 1 teaspoon ground cinnamon
- ½ teaspoon ground nutmeg
- 1/8 teaspoon ground ginger
- 1/8 teaspoon cayenne pepper
- Pinch of sea salt

Directions:

1. In the Instant Pot, place the oil and press "Sauté". Then, add all ingredients except water and cook for about 5 minutes, stirring frequently.
2. Press "Cancel" and stir in water.
3. Close the lid and place the pressure valve to "Seal" position.
4. Press "Manual" and cook under "High Pressure" for about 10 minutes.
5. Meanwhile, preheat the oven to 350 degrees F.
6. Press "Cancel" and allow a "Natural" release for about 10 minutes. Then allow a "Quick" release.
7. Open the lid and transfer the pecans onto a baking sheet.
8. Bake for about 5 minutes.
9. Remove the baking sheet from oven and set aside to cool before serving.

Nutrition:

- Info Per serving:Calories: 162, Fats: 15g, Carbs: 3.8g, Sugar: 1g, Proteins: 6g, Sodium: 14mg

Mushroom Tofu Scramble

Servings: 2
Cooking Time: 7 Minutes

Ingredients:
- 1 cup firm tofu
- 1 cup chopped mixed mushrooms
- 3 tbsps. mushroom soup
- 1 tsp. mixed herbs
- 1 tsp. salt

Directions:
1. Spray a heat-proof bowl that fits in your Instant Pot with nonstick spray.
2. Chop the tofu finely.
3. Mix with the other ingredients. Pour into the bowl.
4. Place the bowl in your steamer basket.
5. Pour 1 cup of water into your Instant Pot. Lower the basket into your Instant Pot.
6. Seal and cook on low pressure for 7 minutes. Depressurize quickly.
7. Stir well and allow to rest, it will finish cooking in its own heat.

Nutrition:
- InfoCalories 120, Carbs 3g, Fat 3g, Protein 18g, Potassium (K) 894 mg, Sodium (Na) 186 mg

Mushroom And Eggs

Servings: 2
Cooking Time: 7 Minutes

Ingredients:

- 4oz egg whites
- 1 cup chopped brown mushrooms
- 2tbsp milk
- zero calorie spray
- 1tsp mustard

Directions:

1. Spray a heat-proof bowl that fits in your Instant Pot with nonstick spray.
2. Whisk together the eggs, milk, and seasoning.
3. Pour into the bowl. Add the mushroom.
4. Place the bowl in your steamer basket.
5. Pour 1 cup of water into your Instant Pot.
6. Lower the basket into your Instant Pot.
7. Seal and cook on low pressure for 7 minutes. Depressurize quickly.
8. Stir well and allow to rest, it will finish cooking in its own heat.

Nutrition:

- Info Per serving:Calories: 80;Carbs: 2 ;Sugar: 0 ;Fat: 1 ;Protein: 15 ;GL: 2

Sweet Potato Fries

Servings: 2

Cooking Time: 15 Minutes

Ingredients:

- 1lb sweet potato, cut into chips.
- 2tbsp butter
- 1tbsp olive oil
- 1tbsp honey
- salt and pepper

Directions:

1. Blanch the potatoes in hot water.
2. Melt the butter and olive oil in the Instant Pot.
3. Add the sweet potato and saute until crisp.
4. Stir in the honey, salt and pepper. Leave to rest.

Nutrition:

- Info Per serving:Calories: 250;Carbs: 36 ;Sugar: 17 ;Fat: 7 ;Protein: 5 ;GL: 30

Cilantro Lime Drumsticks

Servings: 6
Cooking Time: 15 Minutes

Ingredients:

- 1 tbsp. olive oil
- 6 chicken drumsticks
- 4 minced garlic cloves
- ½ cup low-sodium chicken broth
- 1 tsp. cayenne pepper
- 1 tsp. crushed red peppers
- 1 tsp. fine sea salt
- Juice of 1 lime
- To Serve:
- 2 tbsp. chopped cilantro
- Extra lime zest

Directions:

1. Add olive oil to the Instant Pot and set it on the "Sauté" function.
2. Once the oil is hot add the chicken drumsticks, and season them well.
3. Using tongs, stir the drumsticks and brown the drumsticks for 2 minutes per side.
4. Add the lime juice, fresh cilantro, and chicken broth to the pot.
5. Lock and seal the lid, turning the pressure valve to "Sealing."
6. Cook the drumsticks on the "Manual, High Pressure" setting for 9 minutes.
7. Once done allow the pressure to release naturally.
8. Carefully transfer the drumsticks to an aluminum-foiled baking sheet and broil them in the oven for 3-5 minutes until golden brown.
9. Serve warm, garnished with more cilantro and lime zest.

Nutrition:

- InfoCalories 480, Carbs 3.3g, Fat 29 g, Protein 47.2 g, Potassium (K) 677 mg, Sodium (Na) 1180 mg

Eggplant Tofu Scramble

Servings: 2
Cooking Time: 7 Minutes

Ingredients:
- 1 cup firm tofu
- 1 cup roughly chopped eggplant
- 3tbsp low calorie stock
- 1tsp mustard
- pinch of salt

Directions:
1. Spray a heat-proof bowl that fits in your Instant Pot with nonstick spray.
2. Chop the tofu finely. Mix with the other ingredients. Pour into the bowl.
3. Place the bowl in your steamer basket.
4. Pour 1 cup of water into your Instant Pot. Lower the basket into your Instant Pot.
5. Seal and cook on low pressure for 7 minutes. Depressurize quickly.
6. Stir well and allow to rest, it will finish cooking in its own heat.

Nutrition:
- Info Per serving:Calories: 130;Carbs: 5 ;Sugar: 1 ;Fat: 3 ;Protein: 19 ;GL: 1

Spinach Dip

Servings: 2
Cooking Time: 2 Minutes

Ingredients:
- 1oz chopped spinach
- 1oz low fat plain yogurt
- 1tbsp peanut butter
- 1tsp honey
- 1/4tsp chili pepper

Directions:
1. Place the spinach, yogurt, and peanut butter in a heat-proof bowl.
2. Pour a cup of water into the Instant Pot.
3. Place the bowl in the steamer basket and the basket in the Instant Pot.
4. Cook on Stew, low pressure for 2 minutes.
5. Release the pressure quickly.
6. Stir well and add the honey and chili.

Nutrition:
- Info Per serving:Calories: 112;Carbs: 8 ;Sugar: 6 ;Fat: 8 ;Protein: 6 ;GL: 3

Mushroom Tofu Scramble

Servings: 2

Cooking Time: 7 Minutes

Ingredients:
- 1 cup firm tofu
- 1 cup chopped mixed mushrooms
- 3tbsp mushroom soup
- 1tsp mixed herbs
- pinch of salt

Directions:
1. Spray a heat-proof bowl that fits in your Instant Pot with nonstick spray.
2. Chop the tofu finely.
3. Mix with the other ingredients. Pour into the bowl.
4. Place the bowl in your steamer basket.
5. Pour 1 cup of water into your Instant Pot. Lower the basket into your Instant Pot.
6. Seal and cook on low pressure for 7 minutes. Depressurize quickly.
7. Stir well and allow to rest, it will finish cooking in its own heat.

Nutrition:
- Info Per serving:Calories: 120;Carbs: 3 ;Sugar: 1 ;Fat: 3 ;Protein: 18 ;GL: 1

SIDE DISHES RECIPES

Rosemary Potatoes

Servings: 2

Cooking Time: 25 Minutes.

Ingredients:
- 1lb red potatoes
- 1 cup vegetable stock
- 2tbsp olive oil
- 2tbsp rosemary sprigs

Directions:
1. Put the potatoes in the steamer basket and add the stock into the Instant Pot.
2. Steam the potatoes in your Instant Pot for 15 minutes.
3. Depressurize and pour away the remaining stock.
4. Set to saute and add the oil, rosemary, and potatoes.
5. Cook until brown.

Nutrition:
- Info Per serving:Calories: 195;Carbs: 31 ;Sugar: 1 ;Fat: 6 ;Protein: 5 ;GL: 25

Lemon Hummus

Servings: 6
Cooking Time: 40 Minutes

Ingredients:
- 1-pound chickpeas, dried
- 2 lemons, juiced
- 1 tablespoon chopped parsley
- 1 teaspoon minced garlic
- 1/8 teaspoon salt
- 2 tablespoons olive oil
- 1/4 cup tahini paste
- 1/2 of lemon, zested
- 12 cups water

Directions:
1. Plugin instant pot, insert the inner pot, add chickpeas, and pour in water.
2. Shut the instant pot with its lid, turn the pressure knob to seal the pot, press the 'manual' button, then press the 'timer' to set the cooking time to 35 minutes and cook at high pressure, instant pot will take 5 minutes or more for building its inner pressure.
3. When the timer beeps, press 'cancel' button and do natural pressure release for 10 minutes and then do quick pressure release until pressure nob drops down.
4. Open the instant pot, drain chick peas, and transfer to a food processor.
5. Add remaining ingredients except for lemon zest and parsley and pulse chickpeas for 1 to 2 minutes or until smooth, frequently scraping the sides of a food processor.
6. Add water if the hummus is too thick, then tip it in a bowl and garnish with lemon zest and parsley.
7. Serve straight away.

Nutrition:
- InfoCalories: 70 Cal, Carbs: 4 g, Fat: 5 g, Protein: 2 g, Fiber: 1 g.

Chili Lime Salmon

Servings: 2
Cooking Time: 10 Minutes

Ingredients:
- For Sauce:
- 1 jalapeno pepper, deseeded and diced
- 1 tablespoon chopped parsley
- 1 teaspoon minced garlic
- 1/2 teaspoon cumin
- 1/2 teaspoon paprika
- 1/2 teaspoon lime zest
- 1 tablespoon honey
- 1 tablespoon lime juice
- 1 tablespoon olive oil
- 1 tablespoon water
- For Fish:
- 2 salmon fillets, each about 5 ounces
- 1 cup water
- 1/2 teaspoon salt
- 1/8 teaspoon ground black pepper

Directions:
1. Prepare salmon and for this, season salmon with salt and black pepper until evenly coated.
2. Plugin instant pot, insert the inner pot, pour in water, then place steamer basket and place seasoned salmon on it.
3. Shut the instant pot with its lid, turn the pressure knob to seal the pot, press the 'steam' button, then press the 'timer' to set the cooking time to 5 minutes and cook at high pressure, instant pot will take 5 minutes or more for building its inner pressure.
4. Meanwhile, place all the ingredients for the sauce in a bowl, whisk until combined and set aside until required.
5. When the timer beeps, press 'cancel' button and do quick pressure release until pressure nob drops down.
6. Open the instant pot, then transfer salmon to a serving plate and drizzle generously with prepared sauce.
7. Serve straight away.

Nutrition:
- InfoCalories: 305 Cal, Carbs: 29 g, Fat: 5 g, Protein: 36 g, Fiber: 8 g.

Chili Greens

Servings: 2
Cooking Time: 10 Minutes

Ingredients:
- 2 cups mixed cabbage, shredded
- 1 cup trimmed green beans
- 3 stalks chopped scallions
- 2tbsp chili paste
- salt and pepper to taste

Directions:
1. Mix the ingredients in the Instant Pot.
2. Seal and cook on Stew for 10 minutes. Depressurize naturally.

Nutrition:
- Info Per serving:Calories: 60;Carbs: 12 ;Sugar: 1 ;Fat: 0 ;Protein: 2 ;GL: 4

Lemony Brussels Sprouts With Poppy Seeds

Servings: 4
Cooking Time: 2 Minutes

Ingredients:

- 1 pound Brussels sprouts
- 2 tablespoons avocado oil, divided
- 1 cup Vegetable Broth or Chicken Bone Broth
- 1 tablespoon minced garlic
- ½ teaspoon kosher salt
- Freshly ground black pepper
- ½ medium lemon
- ½ tablespoon poppy seeds

Directions:

1. Trim the Brussels sprouts by cutting off the stem ends and removing any loose outer leaves. Cut each in half lengthwise (through the stem).
2. Set the electric pressure cooker to the Sauté/More setting. When the pot is hot, pour in 1 tablespoon of the avocado oil.
3. Add half of the Brussels sprouts to the pot, cut-side down, and let them brown for 3 to 5 minutes without disturbing. Transfer to a bowl and add the remaining tablespoon of avocado oil and the remaining Brussels sprouts to the pot. Hit Cancel and return all of the Brussels sprouts to the pot.
4. Add the broth, garlic, salt, and a few grinds of pepper. Stir to distribute the seasonings.
5. Close and lock the lid of the pressure cooker. Set the valve to sealing.
6. Cook on high pressure for 2 minutes.
7. While the Brussels sprouts are cooking, zest the lemon, then cut it into quarters.
8. When the cooking is complete, hit Cancel and quick release the pressure.
9. Once the pin drops, unlock and remove the lid.
10. Using a slotted spoon, transfer the Brussels sprouts to a serving bowl. Toss with the lemon zest, a squeeze of lemon juice, and the poppy seeds. Serve immediately.

Nutrition:

- Info Per serving: Calories: 125; Total Fat: 8g; Protein: 4g; Carbohydrates: 13g; Sugars: 3g; Fiber: 5g; Sodium: 504mg

Tuna Melt

Servings: 2
Cooking Time: 10 Minutes

Ingredients:
- 8-ounce tuna fillet
- 2 whole-wheat English muffins, halved
- 1 green onion, sliced
- ½ teaspoon ground black pepper
- 1 tablespoon dried dill weed
- 1 tablespoon Dijon mustard
- 3/4 cup Coleslaw mix
- 1 ½ tablespoons mayonnaise
- 1/3 cup grated cheddar cheese
- 1 cup water

Directions:
1. Plugin instant pot, insert the inner pot, pour in water, then insert steamer basket and place tuna on it.
2. Shut the instant pot with its lid, turn the pressure knob to seal the pot, press the 'steam' button, then press the 'timer' to set the cooking time to 4 minutes and cook at high pressure, instant pot will take 5 minutes or more for building its inner pressure.
3. Meanwhile, place remaining ingredients except for cheese and muffins in a large bowl and stir until mixed.
4. When the timer beeps, press 'cancel' button and do natural pressure release for 5 minutes and then do quick pressure release until pressure nob drops down.
5. Open the instant pot, then transfer tuna to a cutting board, let cool for 10 minutes and then shred with two forks.
6. Add shredded tuna to mayonnaise mixture and stir until combined.
7. Cut muffins into half, then top evenly with tuna mixture and sprinkle with cheese.
8. Place muffins under the broiler and cook for 4 to 5 minutes or until cheese melts.
9. Serve straight away.

Nutrition:
- InfoCalories: 306.1 Cal, Carbs: 27.5 g, Fat: 5.5 g, Protein: 35 g, Fiber: 3.8 g.

Quinoa Tabbouleh

Servings: 6

Cooking Time: 16 Minutes

Ingredients:

- 1 cup quinoa, rinsed
- 1 large English cucumber, cut into ¼-inch pieces
- 2 scallions, sliced
- 2 cups cherry tomatoes, halved
- 2/3 cup chopped parsley
- 1/2 cup chopped mint
- ½ teaspoon minced garlic
- 1/2 teaspoon salt
- ½ teaspoon ground black pepper
- 2 tablespoon lemon juice
- 1/2 cup olive oil

Directions:

1. Plugin instant pot, insert the inner pot, add quinoa, then pour in water and stir until mixed.
2. Shut the instant pot with its lid and turn the pressure knob to seal the pot.
3. Press the 'manual' button, then press the 'timer' to set the cooking time to 1 minute and cook at high pressure, instant pot will take 5 minutes or more for building its inner pressure.
4. When the timer beeps, press 'cancel' button and do natural pressure release for 10 minutes and then do quick pressure release until pressure nob drops down.
5. Open the instant pot, fluff quinoa with a fork, then spoon it on a rimmed baking sheet, spread quinoa evenly and let cool.
6. Meanwhile, place lime juice in a small bowl, add garlic and stir until just mixed.
7. Then add salt, black pepper, and olive oil and whisk until combined.
8. Transfer cooled quinoa to a large bowl, add remaining ingredients, then drizzle generously with the prepared lime juice mixture and toss until evenly coated.
9. Taste quinoa to adjust seasoning and then serve.

Nutrition:

- InfoCalories: 283.6 Cal, Carbs: 30.6 g, Fat: 16.1 g, Protein: 5.8 g, Fiber: 3.4 g.

Low Fat Roasties

Servings: 2
Cooking Time: 25 Minutes.

Ingredients:
- 1lb roasting potatoes
- 1 garlic clove
- 1 cup vegetable stock
- 2tbsp olive oil

Directions:
1. Put the potatoes in the steamer basket and add the stock into the Instant Pot.
2. Steam the potatoes in your Instant Pot for 15 minutes.
3. Depressurize and pour away the remaining stock.
4. Set to saute and add the oil, garlic, and potatoes. Cook until brown.

Nutrition:
- Info Per serving:Calories: 201;Carbs: 35 ;Sugar: 1 ;Fat: 6 ;Protein: 5 ;GL: 26

OTHER TYPE 2 DIABETES RECIPES

Poached Peaches

Servings: 4
Cooking Time: 4 Minutes

Ingredients:
- 4 cups of grapefruit juice
- 1 lemon, juice and zest
- 1 cinnamon stick
- 4 peaches, deseeded and peeled

Directions:
1. Pour juice, cinnamon stick, water and lemon juice in the instant pot.
2. Peel the peaches and leave the stem intact. Cut in half and remove the seeds.
3. Now place the peaches in the instant pot.
4. Lock the lid and set the timer to 4 minutes at high pressure.
5. Then, naturally release the steam for 10 minutes, followed by quick release.
6. Open the pot and let the apricots get cooled down. Serve chilled.

Vanilla And Pumpkin Pudding

Servings: 2
Cooking Time: 20 Minutes

Ingredients:
- 2 organic eggs
- 1/2 cup heavy whipping cream
- 3/4 cup stevia
- 16 ounces canned pumpkin puree
- 1 teaspoon vanilla extract

Directions:
1. Grease a small steel pan with oil spray.
2. In a bowl, whisk eggs and then add stevia, cream, canned pumpkin puree, and vanilla extract. Transfer the mixture into the greased pan.
3. Place steaming rack or trivet in instant pot. Pour two cups of water in the instant pot
4. Adjust the pan on the rack.
5. Cover the pan and set the timer to 20 minutes at high pressure
6. Once timer beeps, quick release the steam. Open the instant pot lid.
7. Remove the foil and place steel pan on cooling rack. Chill for 6 hours before servings
8. Enjoy with additional whipping cream

Instant Pot Salmon With Jalapeno

Servings: 2

Cooking Time: 5 Minutes

Ingredients:

- 10 ounces of salmon fillet
- Salt and black pepper, to taste
- 2 jalapeno seeds, minced
- 1 garlic clove
- 2 teaspoons of olive oil
- 1/2 teaspoon cumin

Directions:

1. Combine salt, black pepper, jalapeno seeds, garlic cloves, olive oil and cumin in a bowl.
2. Pour 1-2 cups of water inside the instant pot. Set a steaming rack on top.
3. Cover the steaming rack with aluminum foil. Season the fillet with rub mixture.
4. Place the salmon on the steaming rack.
5. Lock the lid and set the timer to 5 minutes at high pressure.
6. Once the timer beeps, release the steam naturally.
7. Open the lid of the instant pot and then transfer the salmon to plate. Serve and enjoy.

Roasted Tomatillo Salsa

Servings: 1
Cooking Time: 1 Hour

Ingredients:
- 1 pound tomatillos (about 6 large), papery husks removed, rinsed
- ½ large onion, quartered
- 3 serrano chiles, halved lengthwise, seeded
- 1 tablespoon extra-virgin olive oil
- 1 teaspoon kosher salt
- 1 cup (loosely packed) fresh cilantro leaves

Directions:
1. Preheat the oven to 375°F.
2. In an 8-inch square baking dish, combine the tomatillos, onion, chiles, oil, and salt. Roast for 1 hour or until the vegetables are very soft. Remove from the oven and let cool slightly.
3. Transfer everything from the baking dish to a food processor, and add the cilantro. Purée until almost smooth. Pour the salsa into a glass jar and store, covered, in the refrigerator for up to 1 week.

Nutrition:
- Info Per serving(2 TABLESPOONS): Calories: 33; Total Fat: 2g; Protein: 1g; Carbohydrates: 4g; Sugars: 2g; Fiber: 1g; Sodium: 187mg

Herbed Turkey Breast With Butter Gravy

Servings: 2

Cooking Time: 50 Minutes

Ingredients:

- 1.5 pounds of turkey breast
- 1 teaspoon of sage
- ½ teaspoon of thyme
- ¼ teaspoon of dried rosemary
- Salt & pepper
- 1 cup of chicken broth
- ½ cup of butter or oil

Directions:

1. Mix sage, thyme, rosemary, salt and black pepper in a bowl.
2. Rub the turkey meat with the spices. Put the turkey breast in the instant pot.
3. Pour the broth in the instant pot and place lid on top of the instant pot.
4. Set the timer to high for 45 minutes.
5. Once timer beeps, release the steam naturally for 10 minutes.
6. Open the pot and take out the turkey, slice up the turkey breast.
7. Turn on sauté mode and evaporate gravy by adding butter. Serve with turkey.

Keto Instant Pot Chunky Chili

Servings: 2
Cooking Time: 30 Minutes

Ingredients:
- 2 pounds of beef, ground
- 2 tablespoons of olive oil
- 4 garlic cloves, minced
- 1-1/2 cup beef broth
- 1-1/2 cup canned dice tomatoes
- 1 cup zucchini squash, diced

Directions:
1. Turn on the sauté mode of the instant pot. Pour olive oil to the pot and add ground beef.
2. Sauté it for 5 minutes.
3. Once beef is brown, add the garlic cloves, zucchini, and diced tomatoes.
4. Pour the broth and then lock the lid. Set timer for 25 minutes at high pressure.
5. Once timer beeps, release the steam naturally for 10 minutes. Stir and serve.

Chicken Bone Broth

Servings: 8
Cooking Time: 2 Hours

Ingredients:

- 2 or 3 (4-inch) rosemary sprigs
- 2 or 3 (4-inch) thyme sprigs
- 2 or 3 (4-inch) parsley sprigs
- Bones from a 3- to 4-pound chicken
- 1 large onion (unpeeled), root end trimmed, quartered
- 2 large carrots (unpeeled), washed, ends trimmed, and each cut into 4 pieces
- 2 celery stalks (including leaves), ends trimmed and each cut into 4 pieces
- 2 bay leaves
- ⅛ teaspoon black peppercorns
- 1 teaspoon kosher salt (optional)
- 1 tablespoon apple cider vinegar

Directions:

1. Using kitchen twine, tie together the rosemary, thyme, and parsley. (If you don't have any twine, don't worry about it. Tying the herbs together just makes it easier to discard them later.)
2. In the electric pressure cooker, combine the bones, onion, carrots, celery, bay leaves, peppercorns, and salt (if using). Drop the herb bundle on top, then add the vinegar and 8 cups of water.
3. Close and lock the lid of the pressure cooker. Set the valve to sealing.
4. Cook on high pressure for 2 hours.
5. When the cooking is complete, hit Cancel. Allow the pressure to release naturally for 20 minutes, then quick release any remaining pressure.
6. Once the pin drops, unlock and remove the lid.
7. Cool the broth to room temperature, then strain it through a fine-mesh strainer lined with cheesecloth. Discard the solids.
8. Transfer to storage containers and refrigerate for 3 to 4 days, or freeze for up to 1 year.

Nutrition:

- Info Per serving(1 CUP): Calories: 40; Total Fat: 1g; Protein: 6g; Carbohydrates: 3g; Sugars: 0.5g; Fiber: 1g; Sodium: 20mg

Blue Cheese And Pear Melts

Servings: 2
Cooking Time: 2 Minutes

Ingredients:

- 2 ounces cream cheese
- 1/4 cup kiwi, puree
- 2 small pears, thinly sliced
- 4 tablespoons blue cheese, crumbled

Directions:

1. Place the ingredients in the instant pot. Lock the lid.
2. Set the timer to 1-2 minutes at high pressure. Release steam naturally. Stir and serve.

RECIPES INDEX

5-ingredient Mexican Lasagna 48

A
Amaranth Porridge 15
Apple And Cinnamon Cake 81

B
Banana Pancakes 20
Beansprout Soup 25
Beef Goulash 46
Beef With Dried Apricots 14
Blue Cheese And Pear Melts 105
Broccoli Stilton Soup 72
Brownies 76

C
Candied Walnuts 82
Chia Pudding With Mango 78
Chick Pea Curry 29
Chicken & Beans Chili 34
Chicken Bone Broth 104
Chicken Coconut Curry 40
Chicken Stuffed Potatoes 41
Chicken Tacos 32
Chili Con Carne 68
Chili Greens 93
Chili Lime Salmon 92
Chili Sin Carne 61
Cilantro Lime Drumsticks 86
Coconut Cabbage Mix 17
Coconut Shrimp Curry 55
Creamy Broccoli And Ham 28
Crustless Key Lime Cheesecake 74

E
Egg Custard 77
Egg Salad 67
Eggplant Curry 59
Eggplant Tofu Scramble 87
Eggs And Mushroom 19
Eggs And Tomato 13

F
Fabada 43
Fruity Pork Loin 47

G
Glazed Carrots And Cauliflower 27

H
Herbed Turkey Breast With Butter Gravy 102

I
Instant Pot Chicken Breast 36
Instant Pot Cinnamon Apricot And Pears 24
Instant Pot Salmon With Jalapeno 100
Irish Beef Stew 70
Italian Beef Roast 30

K
Kale Sausage Stew 26
Keto Instant Pot Chunky Chili 103
Kidney Bean Stew 65

L
Lamb Chops With Beans & Spinach 42
Lemon Cilantro Chicken 31
Lemon Hummus 91
Lemony Brussels Sprouts With Poppy Seeds 94

Lentil And Eggplant Stew 62
Low Fat Roasties 97

M
Mango Tofu Curry 64
Moroccan Chicken Bowls 37
Mushroom And Eggs 84
Mushroom Tofu Scramble 83
Mushroom Tofu Scramble 89

O
Oatmeal Bites 80
Oats & Millet Porridge 18
Oxtail Soup 45

P
Poached Peaches 98

Q
Quinoa Tabbouleh 96

R
Roast Vegetable And Bean Stew 23
Roasted Tomatillo Salsa 101
Rosemary Potatoes 90
Rosemary Salmon 49

S
Salmon In Green Sauce 56
Sardine Curry 52
Sausage And Cauliflower "grits" 35

Seitan Curry 63
Seitan Roast 60
Shrimp Coconut Curry 53
Shrimp With Tomatoes And Feta 51
Spanish Eggs 16
Spiced Pear Applesauce 73
Spicy Pepper Soup 71
Spinach Dip 88
Split Pea Stew 58
Squash Medley 57
Sweet & Sour Tuna 54
Sweet And Sour Soup 66
Sweet Potato Fries 85
Swordfish Steak 50

T
Thai Green Turkey Curry 39
Tomato Basil Frittata 21
Tuna Melt 95

V
Vanilla And Pumpkin Pudding 99
Vanilla Mug Cake 79
Veal In Milk 44
Vegetables In Half And Half 22

Z
Zucchini Soup 69

Printed in Great Britain
by Amazon